Advance Praise for
The No-Cry Separation Anxiety Solution

"In *The No-Cry Separation Anxiety Solution*, Elizabeth Pantley teaches us the difference between love-based separation anxiety and anxiety that stems from fear. She leaves us knowing that most childhood experiences are healthy, natural stops on the path of development. Through wisdom and many pointers, Elizabeth Pantley will provide this generation with an easier and happier journey through childhood—while also soothing the worry and guilt most parents feel. I'm grateful for this resource and can't imagine raising another child without it."

—*Gavin de Becker, bestselling author of*
The Gift of Fear *and* Protecting the Gift

"Elizabeth Pantley has replaced the angst of separation anxiety with solid practical tips and empathy for both child and parent. Her magical solutions are remarkably easy to implement and result in calm and happy separations for all."

—*Kathy Lynn, president,* Parenting Today,
www.parentingtoday.ca

"*The No-Cry Separation Anxiety Solution* is the perfect read for parents. Not only does Elizabeth Pantley examine and explain separation anxiety, she also provides specific instructions and solutions to help you and your child overcome these challenging moments. Let her imaginative Magic Bracelet work its wonder with your child."

—*Azmina Hansraj, teacher and editor,*
www.baby-mates.com

"Sound, practical advice from America's expert on gentle, thoughtful parenting. Elizabeth Pantley gives many solutions to the rarely discussed problem of separation anxiety. There is something in this book for every family, no matter your parenting style."

—*Robin Elise Weiss, LCCE, author of* The Complete Illustrated Pregnancy Companion *and About.com's pregnancy guide,* http://pregnancy.about.com

"As always, Elizabeth Pantley combines practical ideas and solutions with a deep understanding of how the issue affects everyone in the family. By helping parents to understand separation anxiety as a normal stage of development, she sets a positive stage upon which the scenes of maturity can be played out. Her gentle and reassuring perspective empowers parents to trust their instincts and to nurture their children without forcing independence before they are ready."

—*Nancy Massotto, Ph.D., executive director,* Holistic Moms Network, *www.holisticmoms.org*

the
no-cry separation anxiety solution

*Gentle Ways to Make Good-Bye Easy
from Six Months to Six Years*

Elizabeth Pantley

New York Chicago San Francisco Lisbon London Madrid Mexico City
Milan New Delhi San Juan Seoul Singapore Sydney Toronto

The *McGraw·Hill* Companies

Library of Congress Cataloging-in-Publication Data

Pantley, Elizabeth.
   The no-cry separation anxiety solution : gentle ways to make good-bye easy from six months to six years / by Elizabeth Pantley.
       p.   cm.
   Includes index.
   ISBN-13: 978-0-07-159690-9
   ISBN-10: 0-07-159690-9
   1. Separation anxiety in children.   2. Preschool children—Psychology.   I. Title.

   BF724.3.S38P36   2010
   649'.1—dc22   2009034516

1 2 3 4 5 6 7 8 9 10 11 12 13 14 15 16 17 18   DOC/DOC 1 9 8 7 6 5 4 3 2 1 0

ISBN 978-0-07-174077-7 (book and bracelet set)
MHID   0-07-174077-5 (book and bracelet set)

ISBN 978-0-07-159690-9 (book for set)
MHID   0-07-159690-9 (book for set)

McGraw-Hill books are available at special quantity discounts to use as premiums and sales promotions or for use in corporate training programs. To contact a representative, please e-mail us at bulksales@mcgraw-hill.com.

This book provides a variety of ideas and suggestions. It is sold with the understanding that the publisher and author are not rendering psychological, medical, or professional services. The author is not a doctor or psychologist, and the information in this book is the author's opinion unless otherwise stated. Questions and comments attributed to parents represent complete quotes, compilations, and adaptations of reader letters and test parent letters. This material is presented without any warranty or guarantee of any kind, express or implied, including but not limited to implied warranties of merchantability or fitness for a particular purpose. It is not possible to cover every eventuality in any book, and the reader should consult a professional for individual needs. Readers should bring their child to a medical care provider for regular checkups and bring questions they have to a medical professional. This book is not a substitute for competent professional health care or professional counseling.

DAVID, THIS BOOK IS DEDICATED TO YOU,
in honor of the confident, capable man you have become.
Any mother would be proud to call you son;
I'm glad it's my honor.

Contents

Foreword   ix

Acknowledgments   xi

Editor's Note   xvii

Introduction   xix

1   All About Separation Anxiety in Early Childhood   1

2   No-Cry Solutions for Babies and Toddlers   21

3   The Magic Bracelet Solution for
     No-Cry Separation   41

4   No-Cry Solutions for Preschool and
     School-Age Children   51

5   Solving Specific Separation Situations   81

6   Parents' Separation Anxiety   131

7   Extreme Emotions: Separation Anxiety
     Disorder   141

Index   147

Foreword

As a mother and specialist in the field of early childhood care and education, I have had the opportunity to work with and visit a great many preschool and child-care programs. I know firsthand as a mom, teacher, and administrator what it is like to separate from a young child, even for small portions of the day. While many children are able to transition happily into separation, eager to make new friends and begin new adventures, other children have their safe and secure world rocked by the audacity of Mom or Dad leaving without them, and they show this with heart-wrenching sobs. Once the parent is gone, however, these children readjust and are fine throughout the day, but as soon as Mom or Dad returns, the waterworks start all over again, causing Mom or Dad to feel like the worst parent in the world for leaving the child. There is another group of children who breaks the heart of the parents and the caregiver. This is the child who is truly terrified of being separated from Mom or Dad for even a short period of time, leaving everyone in a daily state of panic.

Even before the age of separation for child care or school, babies and toddlers show their separation distress in ways that cause many parents tremendous worry and concern. Many parents must deal with a crying face at the window, a toddler grasping at their leg, or a baby who clings tightly even in anticipation of separation.

Thank goodness for Elizabeth Pantley and *The No-Cry Separation Anxiety Solution*. Elizabeth helps us to understand what separation anxiety is all about; she reassures us that we are not alone in our need for help and support in raising children who are dealing with separation anxiety; and she powerfully shares her wisdom, experience, and research on the subject throughout the book. She provides a multitude of ideas and solutions that have been tested by her large group of test families. These solutions are presented in ways that can be customized for individual children and include all age groups, from baby to elementary school, so the book can be an ongoing reference for families and professionals.

Moms, dads, caregivers, and child-care providers everywhere will be using and replicating the amazing "magic" of Pantley's No-Cry separation anxiety solutions for years to come.

—Robin Stephenson, M.Ed.
CEO, Professional Early Education Associates
President of the National Association of Child Care Providers

Acknowledgments

I would like to express my sincere appreciation to the many people who make my life easier and happier by providing me with their support in so many ways:

Judith McCarthy, my dedicated, loyal, and encouraging editor.

The entire incredible team of people at McGraw-Hill, including Ann, Donna, Doug, Eileen, Elizabeth, Fiona, Gigi, Greg, Heather, James, Julia, Katherine, Keith, Kenya, Kim, Lizz, Lynda, Marisa, Mary Therese, Pat, Peter, Philip, Robyn, Sally, Shinoa, Sue, Susan, Terrence, Tom, Yin, and those I don't work with directly but whose work I truly appreciate. This amazing team helps to create and market my books, and together we celebrate this tenth book, plus translations into twenty-four languages. I know I have the absolutely best publisher ever.

Meredith Bernstein, of The Meredith Bernstein Literary Agency: friend, counselor, and literary agent extraordinaire.

Patti "The Wonderful" Hughes: my incredible, enthusiastic, do-anything-with-a-smile-and-even-makes-me-cookies assistant.

My husband, Robert: my partner, my friend, and my soul mate for twenty-six blissful years and counting.

My precious children, my ultimate source of joy and inspiration; they make me proud: Angela, Vanessa, David, and Coleton.

My family and my best friends, key to my contentment and happiness: Mom, Michelle, Loren, Sarah, Nicholas, Renée, Tom, Amber, Matthew, Devin, Tyler, Wyatt, Joan, and Rona.

All the readers who have written to me about their dear children. I feel a special friendship with each and every one of you and cherish your letters.

The No-Cry Separation Anxiety group of test mommies, test daddies, and test children. Thank you for sharing a piece of your lives with me: Abigael, Abigail, Adam, Adama, Addisyn, Agnes, Aidan, Ailani, Ainsley, Alannah, Alasia, Alex, Alexander, Alexandra, Alexis, Alfie, Alicia, Allese, Ally, Alyssa, Amanda, Amber, Amy, An,

Ana, Anamarija, Anastasia, André, Andrea, Angela, Angel-lena, Ann, Anna, Annajoy, Anne, Annette, Annika, Ann-Marie, Antalia, Anthony, Antonella, Antonia, Anuradha, April, Ari, Aria, Ariella, Arya Singh, Aspen, Asta, Atlee, Audrey, Aurora, Ava, Balin, Barb, Baxter, Beatrix, Becca, Becka, Bekki, Bella, Benji, Berit, Bianca, Bill, Bonnie, Bowen, Brandel, Brandy, Briana, Bridget, Brighid, Brinley, Caelan, Caitlyn, Caleb, Cameron, Candance, Carla, Carmen, Carol, Caroline, Carolyn, Carrie, Carter, Catherine, Catriona, Cayden, Cesca, Challon, Charles, Charlie, Charlotte, Chaya, Chloe, Christian, Christie, Christina, Christine, Christopher, Christopher II, Cindy, Claire, Cody, Cole, Colten, Connor, Cooper, Corey, Corrine, Cory, Courtney, Cyndi, Cynthia, Dalton, Dani, Daniel, Daniela, Darcie, Darwin, David, Dean, Debbie, Defne, Della, Denise, Deniz, Dominique, Donovan, Dovi, Dylan, Eddie, Édouard, Edurne, Eleanor, Elena, Eli, Eliana, Elisa, Elizabeth, Ellen, Elliot, Emerson, Emily, Emmalee, Emre, Emunah, Eoin, Eran, Erika, Erin, Ester, Esther, Ethan, Eva, Evan, Felicity, Felix, Finley, Fox, Frida, Gabi, Gabrielle, Garrett, Gasper, Gavin, Gay Lynn, Genevieve, George, Giovanni, Gloria, Grace, Graydon, Grayson, Gretchen, Hailey, Haley, Hannah, Hazel, Heather, Hoda, Holden, Hosanna, Ian, Igor, Imke, Isabelle,

Grammy Lee; Laurence, five months old; and Aunt Kathleen

Ivan Luca, Jack, Jackson, Jacob, Jada, Jade, Jakob, James, James Patrick, Jameson, Jamie, Janet, Janie, Jared, Javier, Jayda, Jaylen, Jean Elizabeth, Jekaterina, Jemma, Jen, Jennifer, Jenny, Jeremy, Jessica, Jill, Joanne, Jocelyn, Jodi, Jodie, Joe, Jolene, Jonathan, Josh, Joshua, Juan, Julia, Julian, Julie, Kai, Kara, Kate, Katherine, Katie, Kayleigh, Kelly, Kenya, Kim, Kimberly, Kirsten, Klara, Kristen, Kristin, Kristina, Kristy, Krystal, Kyle, Kyleigh, Kylie, Lana, Lance, Laura, Lauren, Laurence, Lavinia, Layla, Leonie, Lilian, Lilly, Lily, Linda, Lindsay, Lindsey, Lior, Liora, Lis Ana, Lisa, Lisa Marie, Liz, Lochlan, Logan, Lorena, Lorraine, Louise, Lucas, Luka, Luke, Lynn, Maddison, Maddy, Madeleine, Madelyn, Madison, Maeve, Maggie, Marc, Maria, Marjan, Mark, Marta, Martin, Marty, Marwan, Mary, Mary-Anne, Mason, Mati, Matthew, Mattias, Mattie, Megan, Melanie, Melissa, Meridith, Mia, Michael, Michele, Michelle, Milla, Milo, Mina, Mira, Miriam, Molly, Monique, Mordechai, Nahzeer, Nancy, Naomi, Natalie, Natasha, Nathan, Nelle, Nelly, Neve, Nicholas, Nick, Nicole, Nikki, Nina, Noah, Noemi, Oliver, Olivia, Osvald, Owen, Pamela, Patricia, Patrycja, Patti, Patty, Paul, Paula, Petra, Pierce, Pnina, Poppy, Preston, Rachel, Rebecca, Refael, Reme, Rhys, Robin, Rocío, Romi, Rosanna, Rosanne, Ryan, Sabrina, Sadhbh, Sadie, Sakina, Sam, Samantha, Samuel, Sara, Sarah, Sebastian, Şebnem, Seth, Shae, Shane, Shannon, Sharie, Sharon, Shaun, Shaunda, Shea, Shelby, Shirley, Sienna, Sofie, Soleil, Solene, Solveig, Sophia, Sophie, Stella, Stephanie, Stephen, Steven, Steven III, Steven Jr., Stien, Susan, Talie, Tamara, Tammi, Tanya, Tara, Taryn, Taylor, Tera, Thijs, Tiffany, Tim, Timothy, Tracy, Tristan, Trudy, Tyler, Vaishali, Vanesa, Vickie, Vida, Vikki, Vince, Vincent, Virginia, Wendy, Wesley, Weston, William, Wyatt, Xander, Yasmin, Yedidya, Yenny, Yolanda, Yoni, Yonina, Zachary, Zahava, Zavier, Zion, Zita, Živa, Zoe.

The Test Parents

During the creation of this book, I received input, ideas, feedback, questions, and delightful photos from an incredible group of test parents. These 246 people (parents to 358 precious children) let me peek into their families' separation anxiety problems and happy successes.

The No-Cry test parents live all over the world and represent all different kinds of families: parents may be young, older, married, single, unmarried partners, gay partners, or grandparents; both parents may work, or either mom or dad may stay home; families may include one to five children, twins, and/or adopted children, all of various ages; and a family may comprise different races and/or cultures. The test mommies and daddies, as I affectionately call them, became my friends during this long and complicated process, and I believe I learned as much from them as they learned from me. They are a varied and interesting group, as you can see from the following lists:

Locations
- 155 from the United States (Alabama, Alaska, Arizona, California, Colorado, Connecticut, Florida, Georgia, Illinois, Indiana, Iowa, Kansas, Kentucky, Maryland, Massachusetts, Michigan, Minnesota, Missouri, Nevada, New Hampshire, New Jersey, New York, North Carolina, North Dakota, Oklahoma, Oregon, Pennsylvania, Rhode Island, South Carolina, Tennessee, Texas, Utah, Vermont, Virginia, Washington, and Wisconsin)
- 31 from Canada (Alberta, British Columbia, Manitoba, New Brunswick, Nova Scotia, Ontario, Quebec, Saskatchewan, and Yukon)
- 13 from Australia (Adelaide, Albion Park, Bayswater, Canberra, Hawthorn, Jerrabomberra, Melbourne, Mitchell Park, Naremburn, Newman, Perth, Victoria, and Wellington)
- 10 from the United Kingdom (Cornwall, London, Norfolk, Suffolk, and Surrey in England; Edinburgh in Scotland; Cardiff in Wales)
- 7 from South Africa (Capetown, Grahamstown, and Pretoria)
- 3 from Germany (Cologne, Filderstadt, and Munich)
- 2 from Belgium (Lummen and Vosselaar)
- 2 from Israel (Jerusalem and Nof Ayalon)
- 2 from the Netherlands (Urmond and Valkenswaard)
- 2 from New Zealand (Hibiscus Coast)
- 2 from Slovenia (Notranje Gorice)

- 2 from Spain (Palma de Mallorca and Valencia)
- 2 from Sweden (Karlshamn and Olofström)
- 2 from Turkey (Istanbul)
- 1 from Argentina (Ciudad de Buenos Aires)
- 1 from Brazil (Rio de Janeiro)
- 1 from Croatia (Bale)
- 1 from Cyprus (Limassol)
- 1 from Egypt (Cairo)
- 1 from France (Aigrefeuille-sur-Maine)
- 1 from Italy (Pergine)
- 1 from Norway (Oswald)
- 1 from the Philippines (Mandaluyong)
- 1 from Portugal (Estoril)
- 1 from Singapore

Children
- 176 girls
- 182 boys
- 8 sets of twins
- 71 babies (birth to twelve months)
- 169 toddlers (twelve months to three years)
- 82 preschoolers (three years to six years)

Editor's Note

Several years ago, when Elizabeth Pantley came to me with a book idea about helping babies sleep without having to let them cry, I could tell immediately that it was a very special project from a very special author. I knew from my own first-hand experience and from the stories of my equally bleary-eyed friends that it was going to answer the prayers of many, many parents who desperately needed sleep but didn't want to leave their precious little ones screaming in their cribs—that is, *if* Elizabeth could really pull it off.

It turned out she did—even better than I'd hoped—and *The No-Cry Sleep Solution* has been a tremendous gift to more than a million parents and still counting. The outpouring of gratitude to Elizabeth through e-mails, letters, and online comments has been tremendously gratifying to all of us at McGraw-Hill who've had the pleasure of working on the No-Cry books with her. I have had the extra treat of raising my own three children with the sage advice I gain from her books.

In the years since then, Elizabeth's No-Cry approach has helped parents on many other topics as well, from potty training to discipline. But perhaps even more important than these individual topics, as all-consuming as they are when your child is going through them, the No-Cry philosophy helps build strong, loving families—the kind we all want but sometimes need a little help creating. The glowing reviews and appreciative letters from parents continue to praise all the books in the series on this very point. I'm always inspired anew to be the kind of mother I want to be when I go back to reread the books.

Now I'm so pleased that Elizabeth is giving us gentle, No-Cry solutions to separation anxiety. She has pulled it off once again. As with sleep, I know first-hand how painful separation anxiety can be for parents and children. My oldest son had a terrible time when I left to go to work every morning. We muddled our way through many attempts at trying to soothe him—some successful, like always saying good-bye, and some not, like sneaking away to avoid the situation—but I will never forget the wrenching feeling of having to leave the house with my adored child crying at the window. Nor will I forget, a few years later, seeing the pain and frustration of a friend whose child ran and hid behind trees to avoid leaving his mommy to enter the kindergarten classroom.

I am so happy that Elizabeth's solutions, with what we call the Pantley Magic Bracelet as a brilliant spotlight, are helping parents and children to overcome this anxiety more quickly and easily than I would have thought possible. The Magic Bracelet effect truly has to be seen to be believed! Because we are so confident in this approach—and because it's already worked for so many of the test families with whom Elizabeth has worked—we knew we had to include a bracelet with the book so you can get started reducing your own child's separation anxiety right away. We are confident that this book will provide the solutions you need for you and your child. Good luck!

—Judith McCarthy
Editor of the No-Cry series
and Editorial Director,
McGraw-Hill Professional

Introduction

As a mother of four, I've had my struggles with my children's separation anxiety. My oldest daughter was a superglue baby. Angela had such extreme separation anxiety that we waited to hire our first babysitter until she was ten months old. On that momentous day, our leaving was punctuated with an unbearable scene: Angela's tiny little face and hands pressed against the window, tears flowing down her face as we drove off. It broke my heart into a million pieces, and I found it hard to enjoy our time away. An hour after we left, we received a call at the restaurant from the babysitter, asking us to come home. Angela had spent the entire hour crawling away from the sitter—no toy, book, or snack would calm her down—and she was still crying, with no signs of stopping. So we went home. She launched herself into my arms and clung to me as if I were her lifeline. The event was so difficult for her—and us—that for many months thereafter our dinner dates were for three.

When my second daughter, Vanessa, was three years old, we signed her up for preschool. She did not want to go and made her opinion very clear. Every single morning after I dressed her for school, she would hide behind the sofa and get *undressed*, all the while crying that she wanted to stay home. In the car, she'd take off her shoes and socks, her way of telling me she wasn't planning to get out of the car at preschool! When I'd finally redress her and get her into the classroom, she would cling to me and cry, begging me not to leave her. The teachers were kind and sensitive to her needs. "Give it time," they said. "It will get better." It didn't. A month later we unenrolled her from preschool and waited six more months before trying again.

Matthew, my friend's son, was so averse to attending daycare that he panicked every morning as she was leaving for work. He cried nonstop and clung tightly to her when she tried to go. The teacher had to literally pry his little hands off and then hold him tightly so he wouldn't follow his mother out the door. He lost his appetite and began waking up throughout the night. It became an unbearable situation for my friend, so she rearranged her entire life to avoid leaving him. She quit her office job and opened an in-home daycare center so that he wouldn't have to leave her side. He was happy. She was frazzled and frustrated.

I received a letter from Cynthia, a No-Cry book reader who desperately needed help with her daughter Anna's separation anxiety—and with her own as well. Cynthia had never left her child with a babysitter, the gym nursery, a friend, or even her parents. When she left her daughter with her husband (a fabulous and competent daddy), she admitted to feeling sick to her stomach with worry, and she always rushed home. Anna and Cynthia both suffered severe separation anxiety. Anna was soon to celebrate her third birthday. Cynthia was concerned and feeling suffocated by their inability to separate.

My youngest son Coleton's kindergarten year was also a challenging time. Every morning, for the entire first month of school, he complained of a stomachache. I had to coax him out of the car at the curb each day and stuff tissues in his pockets so he could wipe away his tears. I had to walk him to the building . . . to the room . . . to his desk and then quietly and desperately whisper comforting words and promises before I left the room. No matter what I did or said, when I glanced back, I would catch a glimpse of his tear-filled eyes and grief-stricken face as I walked out of the room. His teacher assured me that he did very well once I left, but the knot in my stomach still appeared during this ritualistic morning debacle.

My reader and friend, I know what you're thinking if your child is suffering from separation anxiety, because I have been there too.

But let me give you hope. Allow me to update my previous stories. My firstborn, Angela, eventually *did* accept babysitters, and she had many fun times with them. She now lives on her university campus and babysits for her professor's young daughters. Vanessa did finally make it to preschool and thrived, loving her teachers and making boatloads of friends. She now attends college and has a job as the legislative affairs director for her school, traveling away from home for days at a time.

Matthew's mother applied many of the separation anxiety ideas presented here and eventually returned to work in an office. Matthew handled the change admirably and came to treat his daycare center as a joy-filled second home. Anna is now three and a half and enjoys time with a babysitter once a week while Cynthia and her husband have a night out; plus Anna happily joins the gym nursery twice a week and has regular outings with her grandparents. Cynthia and Anna are now both free to enjoy their time apart as much as they enjoy their time together.

By the time my little Coleton was struggling with kindergarten, I had already written eight parenting books and built an army of test parents all over the world. I put my contacts and research skills to work on his problem and developed the list of solutions provided here, including the Magic Bracelet, which you will learn about in Chapter 3. Coleton's bracelet was the golden ticket for us—it worked like a charm! The remainder of his kindergarten year was a joyful success. He's now a happy, well-adjusted, outgoing third-grader who loves school and is enjoying a weekend sleepover at a friend's home as I write this.

Separation anxiety seeps into children's lives for many reasons and for both brief and extended separations. Infants cry when parents hand them over to a loving relative. Babies sit on the floor outside a bathroom door while anxious mothers try to take very quick showers. Children cry beside babysitters as parents go off to work, suffer through the feelings of missing a parent who is deployed or away on a business trip, and adjust to their parents' divorce (which means they must always leave someone behind). In addition, children must often leave their parents behind as *they* go off: children who must stay alone at the hospital, go away to camp, or, in the case of divorce, leave one parent's home to stay at the other's. And then there are those nightly battles that occur the world over as parents try to convince anxious children to sleep alone all night in their very own beds and in their very own bedrooms.

This is the book I wish I'd had from the beginning of my parenting career for all the times my four children suffered from separation anxiety, as well as to help *me* with my separation anxiety as I dealt with my own feelings at each of my children's milestones. I am very happy to be able to present these many gentle, effective No-Cry separation anxiety solutions to you, so that you and your child can part ways with a good-bye, a happy wave, and a smile.

1

All About Separation Anxiety in Early Childhood

Separation anxiety: A child's apprehension or fear associated with his or her separation from a parent or other significant person.
—*Stedman's Medical Dictionary*

The origin of separation anxiety is love, so handling it should be done with care and respect. The problems presented by separation anxiety are complex. They can interfere with daily life and create a cloud over the joy of early childhood, bringing many tears from children and much frustration for parents and caregivers. Separation anxiety is a complicated emotion, so it requires knowledge and skill to correctly interpret and adequately solve it.

When we first hold our new babies, we don't know them, but we love them. They don't know us, but instinct tells them we are significant. Every action and every word from that first moment of meeting brings us closer together. Over time, our bond grows, and our love matures. We become important to each other. This bond becomes human glue, and the longer it stays together, the more permanent the hold. We parents work hard to create such an attachment in our early relationship with our children, and we feel an unparalleled joy when we are rewarded with evidence of this bond—a toothless smile just for us, a running leap into our waiting arms, a spontaneous hug, a sunshiny giggle at a private joke. These are the rewards of a well-nourished relationship.

Our children, in their trusting innocence, drink in this special relationship as an integral part of their world. Our presence becomes a regular part of life, as normal as breathing air. Our existence comes to represent normalcy and safety and tells our children that all is well in their world.

But what happens when this safety net is removed? What happens when a parent walks away from a child, leaving him in the hands of someone less familiar? The child suffers a sense of unease, loss, and worry, and he desperately attempts to hold on to the person he feels delivers his peace of mind. The result is a common scene at any day-care, playground, family gathering, or birthday party: a crying child clinging tightly to a parent who is desperately trying to convince that child to let go and join the fun.

Almost all children have some aspect of separation anxiety during the first six years of life. It's a very normal and predictable response to the threatened removal of the most important thing in your child's life: you.

Figuring out how to handle your child's separation anxiety can cause you confusion and frustration. Yet you should not fear it or even wish it away, as it is the most obvious and identifiable sign of your child's love for and trust in you. It is the grand indicator that your child believes that you represent the ultimate in safety, protection, and security above anyone or anything else in this world.

Key Point
In your child's eyes, you are a superhero.

The Reason for Separation Anxiety

It makes perfect sense that children experience separation anxiety when pulled away from their main caregiver, in ways even beyond the primary love emotion. Human beings are wired to respond to fear, perceived danger, or stress with a *fight-or-flight* reaction. This basic response is obviously unachievable for babies and young children who do not have the physical or mental ability to flee or defend themselves. They must rely on trusted adults to protect them from dangers of all kinds. Therefore, "fight or flight" is replaced with an intense need to keep Mommy, Daddy, or Main Caregiver close by to provide protection. This instinctual pull demonstrates a child's perception that his parents are his safeguard against possible threats to his safety, both physical and emotional. The more stress or worry a child feels, the closer he wishes to stay to his parents. This need becomes obvious when a child is placed in a stranger's arms, when he must confront a new situation, or when he is tired or ill.

As a child matures, he learns more about the world and how it works. When he has had multiple experiences of happy partings, safe separations, and subsequent joyful reunions, he eventually realizes that he can relinquish the safe anchor of Mom or Dad and venture farther away without risking a dangerous or troublesome situation. This maturity is not something that you can rush or teach. It must develop over time and with age and experience.

Professional-Speak

"You don't really understand human nature unless you know why a child on a merry-go-round will wave at his parents every time around—and why his parents will always wave back."

—William D. Tammeus, Pulitzer Prize–winning journalist

What Causes Separation Anxiety?

Separation anxiety does not have a precise "cause." It is a perfectly normal and important developmental adaptation of a child's emotional and mental growth. Nothing you have done has "made" your child develop separation anxiety, and nothing you could do would have prevented it in its entirety.

Even though separation anxiety has not been caused by any particular event, certain caregiver actions can either heighten or reduce a child's normal anxiety. Many things can help build your child's growing trust in his world and his confidence in his relationship with you, so that he can transfer these feelings to other adults who will then help him feel safe when he is away from home base.

Nearly all children experience some aspect of separation anxiety at some point in their lives. For some, the stage begins early, at just a few months of age. For others, the effects begin later in life, even after a history free from this problem. Some children have anxiety that lasts for a short blink and disappears quickly and easily, while others have longer spells that seem to build to a peak and then fade away, only to reappear again. Some children give very visible, intense, or obvious indicators of their feelings, but others' reactions are less apparent. There is no exact pattern, although there are typical signs and symptoms at various ages.

The development of separation anxiety indicates that your child is developing intellectually. She has learned that she can have an effect on her world when she makes her needs known, and she doesn't have to passively accept a situation that makes her nervous or uncomfortable. She doesn't know enough about the world yet to understand that when you leave her you'll always come back or that other adults are capable of meeting all her needs, as you do. She does realize that she is safest, happiest, and best cared for with you, so her reluctance to part from you makes perfect sense—especially when viewed from a survival standpoint. Put another way, you are her source of nourishment, both physical and emotional; therefore, her attachment to you is her means of survival, and when she reaches a certain level of intellectual maturity, she realizes this.

This stage, like so many others in childhood, will pass. In time, your child will learn that she *can* separate from you, that you *will* return, and that everything will be okay between those two points in time.

What Determines a Child's Level of Separation Anxiety?

Even though most children show signs of separation anxiety at some point in their lives, you cannot predict how or when yours will demonstrate it. The timing and intensity of any individual child's signs and symptoms vary, depending on a number of factors, including the following:

- The consistent availability of a secondary caregiver with whom the child has a familiar relationship and a loving bond
- The familiarity of the location and situation in which you leave her
- The number and quality of previous separation experiences
- Cultural norms (what is typically done in the society in which she lives)
- Family routines (what is normal for her primary home and extended family)
- The child's temperament and personality
- The parent's personality and parenting style

What Is Stranger Anxiety?

Stranger anxiety is a form of separation anxiety that directly relates to people rather than places or actions. It is based in the same emotions that surround separation anxiety—the fact that a child's main caregivers represent safety and security, and unfamiliar people represent fear of the unknown. The anxiety is caused by the child's inability to predict what the stranger is about: *What will this person do or say? What is this person's place in my world? Will this person take me away from my mother, father, or familiar caregiver? Can this person take care of me? Will this person endanger me or keep me safe?*

Your infant may be outgoing and smile at everyone who talks to her. A few months pass, and suddenly she has a drastic change in reaction to new people. She'll cling to you and cry if a stranger even so much as says hello! What happened to your confident baby? She's reached an important milestone in human development. She is demonstrating that you've done a great job taking care of her. The stranger anxiety your baby is experiencing is a testimony to the strength of her attachment to you.

At What Age Does Stranger Anxiety Normally Appear?

Attachment and bonding, the two components of stranger and separation anxiety, begin to develop right from birth. A newborn enters the world with no understanding of the people in it. During months two through six, your baby learns general rules about people. In most cases, those rules demonstrate that people respond to his needs with those things he requires to survive and thrive. Between months five and nine, sometimes earlier, a baby begins to clearly differentiate between people. She begins to identify familiar people, and all the rest become—*strangers*. Babies respond differently to this revelation, some displaying curiosity, some expressing caution, and some having an intense aversion to anyone beyond the most familiar circle of family. All of these reactions are normal; so are most variations of these extremes.

How Long Does Stranger Anxiety Last?

Many professionals state that stranger anxiety peaks at between twelve and eighteen months and then tapers off. But my research tells me that it seldom disappears so early or so easily. Frequently, children go through spurts of separation and stranger anxiety up until age seven or eight. This anxiety looks different at different ages, and the leap from stranger anxiety to outgoing social butterfly isn't an overnight event; it is a process.

Your child may seem rather unpredictable and moody—sometimes accepting a new person as a potential friend, other times hiding his face in your shoulder if someone tries to engage him in conversation, and sometimes melting down in tears if someone tries to hold or touch him. Over time, he will begin to learn that talking to new people is a safe endeavor and usually a fun thing to do, and he'll wel-

Stella, two years old

come meeting someone new. Keep in mind that this transition takes longer for some children than others, and your patience is important as he works though this stage in his life.

What Can I Do to Help My Baby Through This Stage of Development?

Although stranger anxiety is normal and healthy, and although it may linger for quite some time, it's still a good idea to help your child move through this phase. Life is more fun if she can learn to be comfortable with new people. It can help you to shift your child's way of thinking from separation as a process of moving *away* from you to separation as a step *toward* connection with other human beings.

The ideas in this book address all aspects of separation anxiety, which includes the subset of stranger anxiety, because it's sometimes hard to differentiate between the two. Therefore, most of the ideas presented here will help your child adapt in situations of both separation anxiety and stranger anxiety.

How Do I Know if My Child Has Separation Anxiety?

Separation anxiety has many different symptoms, but it is often easy for parents to spot in their own child. The following behaviors are most typically used to define normal separation anxiety:

- Clinginess
- Crying when a parent is out of sight
- A strong preference for one parent over all other human beings
- Fear of strangers or of family or friends who are not frequently seen
- Resistance to separation at bedtime or naptime
- Waking at night crying for a parent
- Regression to an earlier stage of development (such as thumb sucking, toileting accidents, baby talk)
- Anxiety that dissipates quickly when a parent appears

Father-Speak

"I was really worried about our son. He clings to his mother constantly. If she leaves the room, he wails and screams as if she's left the country. When I mentioned this to the other dads at my daughter's baseball game, I heard that their kids all did the same thing at one time or another. Since I learned that it's normal, I'm no longer alarmed at his behavior."

—Adam, father of one-year-old Seth and six-year-old Claire

Children are unique in their personalities, yet they are often similar in many ways when it comes to displaying characteristics of anxiety. I surveyed my group of 246 test parents to learn more about the symptoms their children experienced. The following chart summarizes what they said.

Separation Anxiety Signs, Symptoms, and Behaviors*

Symptoms/Signs	Age	Usually exhibits	Sometimes exhibits	Never exhibits**	Total exhibiting signs
Cries when parent leaves the room	6–11 months	25%	38%	12%	63%
	12 months–2 years	5%	21%		26%
	2–3 years	3%	11%		14%
	3–5 years	2%	5%		7%
Cries when parent leaves the house	6–11 months	33%	18%	18%	51%
	12 months–2 years	11%	27%		38%
	2–3 years	5%	11%		16%
	3–5 years	2%	6%		8%
Clings to parent	6–11 months	33%	29%	9%	62%
	12 months–2 years	8%	20%		28%
	2–3 years	5%	10%		15%
	3–5 years	3%	7%		10%
Follows parent from room to room	6–11 months	28%	19%	9%	47%
	12 months–2 years	7%	22%		29%
	2–3 years	5%	9%		14%
	3–5 years	4%	4%		8%
Fears strangers	6–11 months	13%	21%	56%	34%
	12 months–2 years	8%	10%		18%
	2–3 years	6%	9%		15%
	3–5 years	2%	6%		8%

continued

*As indicated by test parents who completed the survey
**Includes all age groups

The No-Cry Separation Anxiety Solution © Better Beginnings, Inc.

Separation Anxiety Signs, Symptoms, and Behaviors* (continued)

Symptoms/Signs	Age	Usually exhibits	Sometimes exhibits	Never exhibits**	Total exhibiting signs
Acts shy around strangers	6–11 months	31%	20%	15%	51%
	12 months–2 years	7%	19%		26%
	2–3 years	7%	14%		21%
	3–5 years	6%	12%		18%
Prefers mother to everyone else	6–11 months	52%	21%	13%	73%
	12 months–2 years	16%	10%		26%
	2–3 years	11%	8%		19%
	3–5 years	4%	9%		13%
Refuses to fall asleep without a parent present	6–11 months	53%	19%	24%	72%
	12 months–2 years	18%	31%		49%
	2–3 years	17%	21%		38%
	3–5 years	9%	16%		25%
Won't leave parent's side at playground, public place, or playmate's home	6–11 months	12%	14%	59%	26%
	12 months–2 years	9%	19%		28%
	2–3 years	5%	11%		16%
	3–5 years	3%	9%		12%

*As indicated by test parents who completed the survey
**Includes all age groups

The No-Cry Separation Anxiety Solution © Better Beginnings, Inc.

I asked the test parents to pick words to describe *their emotions* over their child's separation anxiety. Following are the percentage of respondents picking a particular word:

90% Frustration
70% Sadness
70% Sympathy
60% Confusion
60% Concern
50% Worry
40% Anger
30% Embarrassment
20% Irritation
15% Acceptance

Separation Anxiety Is Fluid

Separation anxiety doesn't have a specific beginning nor does it have an exact end. It doesn't build in predictable, identifiable ways. It shows itself in peaks and valleys—good days and bad days, good weeks and bad weeks, and even good years followed by bad weeks. Separation anxiety has common themes and typical symptoms, but it shows up differently in every child.

It can be bewildering to parents when their child shifts from confidence to anxiety and back again many times during the growing-up years, but this unpredictable behavior is actually very normal. Gaining the maturity and skills to handle many different kinds of separation with confidence is a process, not a single event.

Professional-Speak

"A preschooler's unwillingness to leave a parent or other beloved adult is a good sign that important attachments have developed. Many experts believe this capacity is a prerequisite for a healthy personality and a satisfying adulthood."

—The National Parent Information Network

Is Something Wrong if a Child *Doesn't* Have Separation Anxiety?

Some children seem to learn early on that any adult can provide the safety and security they need. These kids are remarkably flexible and don't present any separation anxiety problems. They adapt seamlessly from one new experience to another and make friends of all ages easily. The biggest issue with these fearless kids is teaching them enough "Stranger Danger" lessons to prevent them from wandering off with a friendly stranger at the park or shopping mall.

Some children don't have any outward demonstration of separation anxiety—but they have the feelings nonetheless. While crying, clinging children can be a frustration, silent, suffering children can present a real challenge, since their anxiety can simmer quietly or in ways that are harder to identify.

Almost all children feel some anxiety when facing a new situation, just as all adults feel some anxiety when starting the first day at a new job or moving into a new neighborhood. Therefore, it can be helpful to read over the ideas presented in this book and apply some of the solutions even with a child who doesn't present any obvious

Daddy Kariem and Kairo, sixteen months old

need. For example, having a specific good-bye routine is helpful to all children, regardless of their anxiety status.

If you have more than one child, it is highly possible that they are all different: you may have one child who has no anxiety, one who has silent symptoms, and yet another who exhibits many outward signs of anxiety. This is a character personality trait that is inborn and then shaped by various outside influences, only some of which originate with parents. So in a family with many children, you often see varying degrees and types of anxiety among them. That's why it is critical for parents and caregivers to examine each individual child's needs, so they can give whatever help that particular child needs to combat feelings of separation anxiety.

Keep Your Child Emotionally Safe

Parents can become entrenched in their own interpretation of their child's behavior. They witness outrageous behavior—like screaming or tantrums over seemingly ridiculous events, such as a visit from a loving grandparent—and don't really understand what's happening. It can help to consider the situation from a child's point of view:

- Children don't *choose* to have separation anxiety.
- Children don't enjoy having separation anxiety.
- Children wish they didn't have separation anxiety.
- Children don't know how to get rid of their separation anxiety.

Separation anxiety is a feeling that comes on children unbidden and won't leave easily. Since the feelings are there, it's a helpful beginning for your child to know that you understand. It can be reassuring to your child to know that what he feels is normal and that you love him and believe in him even when he struggles, even when he cries, and even when his behavior makes your life difficult.

There are times, of course, when your frustration will show itself in your words and actions; you are human too, after all. Forgive yourself those mistakes and work on sending an overall message of love, support, and acceptance of his feelings. That doesn't mean you should allow your child to control your life with his anxious behavior, nor does it mean you shouldn't try to help him let go when he needs to. It means that when you do, you are sensitive and kind in the way you approach his feelings.

If Separation Anxiety Is a Sign of Love and Security, Should I Force Separation?

Separations represent developmental opportunities, but they are only one piece of the massive jigsaw puzzle that is early childhood. Any one separation situation does not make or break your child for life. Any one time that you choose to proceed or to bypass a situation of separation does not create a lifetime affect. It is the accumulation of many such situations that takes your child on a journey from being a totally dependent and attached newborn all the way to his wedding day.

Timing is important when you forge ahead with separation. There are moments when pushing for separation serves no productive purpose and simply creates a flood of upset in the family. Other times are ripe for new separation situations, and while they may start out shaky, they blossom into wonderful learning experiences.

By gently encouraging your child's separation confidence at the right times and in the right ways, you can teach him valuable life lessons like these:

- How to find ways to control his emotions in difficult situations
- How to handle his emotions about missing the people that he loves
- How to know that people love him even when they are not with him
- How to use positive self-talk to convince himself to do things even when he has worries
- How to persist in unfamiliar or uncomfortable situations despite emotional challenges or fears
- How to use past successes as evidence that he is capable of overcoming fears and forging ahead
- How to accept that he is good company for himself

Emotions and Situations That Masquerade as Separation Anxiety

A number of emotions and situations can make it seem that your child is suffering from separation anxiety because the symptoms are similar. It's helpful to review the following list to determine if any of these situations fit your child's experiences. It is possible that your child could have *both* the described emotion *and* separation anxiety, but only you can determine the part that such situations play in your child's case. It is easy to misread a child's response, so you can make the most accurate determination by keeping an open mind.

- **Lifestyle changes.** A change in a child's way of life might bring about symptoms that appear to be separation anxiety but really aren't. For example, while fear of sleeping alone can be a symptom of separation anxiety, not all children who are afraid to sleep alone actually have separation anxiety. Children who have regularly co-slept with their parents or siblings may simply be accustomed to sleeping with another person and find it unsettling when they are required to sleep alone. Ideas for moving from co-sleeping to independent sleep can be found on my website (www.nocrysolution.com) or in any of my No-Cry books on the topic of sleep.
- **Lack of experience or slow adaptation.** If your child has never been left with a babysitter, never experienced a playdate, or had little exposure to new people, then these situations can rightly cause some uncertainty. In these cases, you are dealing with a lack of familiarity rather than separation anxiety, and practice plus patience during the adjustment is what is most required.
- **Shyness.** When your preschooler hides his face in your side and refuses to say a polite "hello" to your friend, your toddler turns away from the cheerful cashier offering a free sticker, or your baby cries when an unfamiliar aunt tries to pick her up, you may attribute this behavior to separation anxiety or stranger anxiety. However, it may just be a shy child who is uncomfortable around new people or who is more reserved or slower to warm up in social situations.
- **Fear.** A child who clings tightly to you if you try to leave him alone in a dark bedroom, a toddler who refuses to leave your side to climb on the playground toys, or an older child who refuses to join

a sports team or ride his bike to school—these are all examples of children who may have fears that appear to be separation anxiety. Fear of the dark, monsters, the unknown, or being hurt can make it appear that your child doesn't want to separate from you, but what he's looking for is protection from the object of his trepidation—and that protection is you. By helping him find ways to feel safe as he ventures out into the world, you can help him overcome these fears.

• **Worry.** Your child may hear a news story about an airplane crash, a missing person, a war, or another disaster. He might talk to a friend whose parents recently divorced or whose grandparent passed away. At these times, he may suddenly find that he can't control his worries about you when you are out of sight—so his solution is to stay by you at all times. If this is your situation, talk to your child about his concerns. Explain all the steps you take to keep yourself safe. Allow him to call you or send a text message when possible. If you stay calm and reassuring, this phase should pass.

• **Embarrassment.** Your previously happy kindergartener suddenly begs to stay home from school. Your preschooler won't leave your side to ask the librarian she's talked to many times before to help her find a book. Your grade-schooler refuses to answer a simple "How are you?" from a neighbor. In these cases, embarrassment or awkwardness may be to blame.

Ask a few "why" questions to determine if something has happened to make your child feel uncomfortable. Perhaps someone laughed at a question she asked, or she got lost on the way back from the school library to her classroom. If you can learn what is causing the embarrassment, you can bring it out into the open. When you provide reassurance that her experience is normal and help her with tips on how she can overcome her feelings, you can move her past the discomforting incident.

Is Your Child's Separation Anxiety Really a Problem?

There are times when children must separate from their parents, but there are also times when separation is *optional.* I have never seen any

Mother-Speak

"I'm a teacher and on a school holiday break I wanted to spend the extra time with my son, but due to advice from others, I decided to leave him in daycare. Friends told me how lucky I was to have this 'time to myself.' I really struggled with dropping Luke off and was nearly overwhelmed with feelings of sadness—and some guilt too. I felt like all the things that I'd planned to do seemed a bit pointless. I didn't really enjoy the 'time off' at all, so I ended up changing plans and keeping him with me. It was a glorious week for both of us. Now I'll be much more careful about automatically taking others' advice about what's right for us."

—Mother of three-year-old Luke

studies that support pushing a parent-child partnership to separate just for the sake of personal growth. Every child is unique, and every family is the only one of its kind. The treatment of separation anxiety should require an individual decision for each child and for each situation.

This book, like all my No-Cry parenting books, is about solving those problems that *you* feel are problems. Every family views separation anxiety issues differently. Just because there is a chapter about how to help your baby accept a babysitter, it doesn't mean you have to hire one. If you are happy taking your baby along with you on your night out—then go right ahead and do that. Just because there is a chapter about how to help your child adjust to daycare, it doesn't mean that every child should attend daycare; it means that *if* your child is struggling in this area and you'd like to help him adjust and become happy in the situation, *then* I will provide you with ideas to help you make that change. On the other hand, if you decide that it's best to pass on daycare for now and simply keep your child at home with you, then that may be *your* best solution. Many children bypass the daycare experience—and some even bypass the preschool experience—yet go on to be perfectly well-adjusted and happy kids with lots of friends once they begin kindergarten. I know because I had one of those children!

Braedon, six months old

As part of the process, consider why you feel the issue needs to be solved. Is this truly something that must be addressed for your child's emotional growth? Is this situation the absolute best one for everyone in the family? Are you considering changes because of your own memories of childhood, input from outsiders, or worries about potential problems, or is this something that is truly affecting your child and must be addressed now?

There's a flip side to outside influences as well. It comprises the other half of the population, who feels you are making the wrong decision when you address your child's anxiety by doing what's necessary to move her forward. Once you have decided it's time to let your child take a separation step, whether it's going to camp, a playdate, or daycare, you should never accept guilt-inflicting comments that encouraging your child's separation is a bad thing or that you are being selfish or neglectful! It is a wonderful thing to help your child become more independent. And it's great to be able to go on a date night, take a class, go to work, have lunch with friends, or use the bathroom all by yourself, and leave your child in the care of another loving, competent adult. Your child can blossom while in the care of someone other than you. There is an added benefit for your child—the value of learning how to interact with many different kinds of people outside your immediate family.

There are no cookie-cutter solutions to any parenting problem, including separation anxiety. I will provide an assortment of ideas for you to choose from for each situation. Pick one, pick two, or combine a variety of ideas to create a personalized plan for your child. Then adjust and modify your plan as you go until you find the right solution. That's how the process of raising children works best.

With this important concept in mind, let's start with a crucial principle that I urge you to keep as a guiding light throughout the rest of this book—and for that matter, the rest of your life. This concept can be applied to almost any parenting decision you'll face from now through grandchildren, and even your *great*-grandchildren.

 The No-Cry Process for Peaceful Problem Solving

There are no absolute rules about raising children and no guarantees for any parenting techniques. Raise your children as you choose to raise them in ways that are right for you. Within the range of your comfort zone, modify your approach for each of your children based on their needs, personality, and temperament.

Address only those problems that you believe are true problems, and don't create or imagine problems because someone else thinks you have them, no matter if that person is family, friend, or expert.

Keep your problems in perspective and take ample time to plot the best course of action. Solve your problems by analyzing possible solutions and choosing those that are right for you and your family. Know that there is rarely one right answer, and often you must take multiple routes to get to the best destination.

Read, listen, and learn constantly, but always sift what you learn through the strainer of your own personal beliefs and parenting philosophy.

Mother-Speak

"Luke was a mega-attached baby. I couldn't leave him with a babysitter, couldn't leave his side at the park, or couldn't leave the room without him melting down. Heck, I couldn't even use the bathroom without having him by my side! People told me I was being oversensitive to his needs and I should let him grow up—which seemed ridiculous to me. Since when is it necessary for a baby to be in a rush to grow up? Especially when so much of what I've done in his life has been to create a strong bond between us. That bond is worth its weight in gold to me.

"Yet I still found I wanted to have a dinner out with adults or go for a jog without pushing the stroller. I didn't know how to achieve this without Luke crying. So I figured I'd go to the No-Cry expert for advice, and I'm so glad I did!

"Since I've been working on the ideas you gave me, I've changed my approach. I've been patient and responsive to his cues, but I've also started giving him space when the opportunity presents itself. We've played the separation games. I have taken things step-by-step, with lots of reassurance. I carefully present him with new situations, explain them beforehand, and then ease him into them gradually. I recently gave Luke his very own Magic Bracelet when he went overnight to his grandmother's house, and it was truly magic. They had a great time—with no crying!

"I have to tell you that Luke is so secure now that he's counting off the days until preschool starts on the wall calendar, and he happily goes off to the health club daycare—and anywhere else, for that matter, anytime he's invited. He's become quite a social butterfly. Now I'm the one having separation anxiety!"

—**Gloria, mother of four-year-old Luke**

2

No-Cry Solutions for
Babies and Toddlers

From the time that babies become aware of the world around them, they begin to form important relationships with the people in their lives. They quickly learn that certain people are vital to their happiness and survival. Babies and toddlers don't have the ability to understand how the world works, so they don't know what makes these people appear or disappear, and when they are out of sight, the little ones have no way of knowing if their beloved people are gone forever. Babies and toddlers crave the nearness of those they love, so to protect themselves from potential loss, they use the only methods they have available to them to express their feelings: they cry and they cling.

Try to embrace separation anxiety as a positive sign. It's perfectly okay—even wonderful—for your child to be so attached to you and for her to desire your constant companionship. It's evidence that the bond you've worked so hard to create is holding. So politely ignore those who tell you otherwise.

Over time, your little one will learn that when the two of you are separated everything is just fine and other people are capable of meeting her needs. She'll also learn through experience that you always return eventually. It will take time, however, for your child to mature enough to reach this point. Until then, to help her learn to understand, accept, and deal with separation, try some of the following ideas.

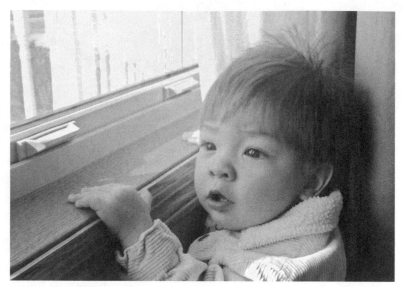

Alex, nine months old

Play Peek-a-Boo with Objects

This time-honored game is a great way to teach your baby an important concept that will allow him to begin to understand the foundation of separation: things exist even if he can't see them, and when they go, they come back. This will be helpful when it's *you* that is gone and cannot be seen. Take an opportunity during playtime to hide toys under blankets or containers and then pull them back out again with a flourish. When you put something under a blanket, you can sometimes let your baby feel it from the top to show that the object is still there. Or put something in a jar and rattle it around, then slowly pull it out little by little. Let your baby have a turn with the toy hiding too, and then you can find it with a joyful hurrah.

A great variation on this game is to use a toy house and toy people and show them going in and out and around. Get creative here and show them driving off in a car, going to the office or grocery store or wherever you go when you leave the house. Always have a pleasant good-bye and a happy moment when they arrive back home. Play the game often for the best learning effect.

Play Peek-a-Boo with People

Parents seem to play this game instinctually, and it's more than just for fun, it's an important lesson for your baby. One step beyond peek-a-boo with toys, this game actually demonstrates that people still exist even when you can't see them—and that they do return and it's fun when they come back.

There are many ways to play. You can hide your face behind your hands or a blanket, or even behind your baby's legs during diaper changes. Stay hidden for a few seconds, and then you might ask, "Where's Mommy?" Pause while your baby processes the question and then pop out and cheerfully announce, "Peek-a-boo! Here I am!" Over time, hide more of your face and then hide for longer periods of time. You can also use an object to cover your baby's face ("Where's Baby?") and then let *him* be the one to pop out.

> **Father-Speak**
>
> "I discovered that the games we have been playing with Maddie are working. I went out to the store for an hour, and when I came back, she bounced up, threw up her arms, and yelled, 'Peek-a-boo!' just like she does when we play the game."
>
> **—Mark, father of nineteen-month-old Madison**

Play the Bye-Bye Game

This game expands object permanence lessons to include the typical words and gestures we use when leaving and returning. It helps your baby learn the concepts of "hello" and "bye-bye" and demonstrates what these phrases represent.

This is how to play: Say, "Bye-bye" (or whatever words or phrases you typically use when leaving your child) and duck behind a corner or a piece of furniture. A few seconds later, pop out and say, "Hi!" (or your usual welcoming phrase). Continue to play this game daily—staying hidden for longer periods of time. You can expand the game to include times when you leave the room to shower, do laundry, or make dinner. You can also let your baby have a turn at hiding. Once your little one is used to the coming and going and the typical gestures and phrases you use, then it should make your actual separations a little bit easier.

Practice with Quick, Safe Separations During the Day

Over the course of your usual days together take opportunities to expose your baby to a few brief, safe visual separations. This process is particularly useful for the little superglue children who need you to be within arm's reach at all times.

Begin by getting your child interested in a toy, a game, or another person. When your little one is happily engaged in play, walk away slowly, and go briefly into another room. Whistle, sing, hum, or talk as you go and when you are out of sight so that she knows you're still there, even though she can't see you. If she seems nervous at first, then stay away just for a moment and slowly expand the times you step out.

Carry out these brief separations off and on throughout the day in a variety of different situations. Start with just a few minutes and gradually build the length of separation time. (Never leave a child unsupervised, unless she is in a child-safe location, like a crib, and even then, just for short periods of time.)

Avoid an In-Arms Transfer

It's common to hand a baby from one caregiver to another. The problem with this is that your little one is leaving the safety and warmth of your arms and being physically whisked away to another, less-familiar person. This type of parting is almost physically painful for children. It is the ultimate separation anxiety producer.

To avoid the arms-to-arms transfer, make the change with your baby situated in a neutral place, such as playing on the floor or sitting in a swing, high chair, or baby seat. Have the other caregiver sit next to your baby and engage her attention as you say a quick, happy good-bye and leave. As soon as you are gone is the best time for the caregiver to pick up your child. The advantage here is that the caregiver will be put in the position of rescuer—and that can help build his relationship with your baby.

Don't Be Afraid of Babying Your Baby

It is honorable and considerate for you to respect your child's needs. Separation anxiety is a biologically necessary emotion and a sign of deep love and attachment. All children move through this phase in their own way and on their own timetable. Pushing your child to separate from you despite his protests is not a productive way to encourage his independence and, in fact, might exacerbate the situation, making your child even more fearful to part from you.

Mother-Speak

"If my son doesn't want to be separated from me, it is for a reason, and I am happy to meet the needs that he has. He is only two years old! In the blink of an eye, he will be a big boy who doesn't want Mummy around. Although I find separation anxiety hard to deal with, I don't see it as a permanent state of being. He is only going to be little for a while, and if he needs all of me right now, he can have me."

—Lana, mother of two-year-old Lior

Permit your child to slowly develop independence on his own schedule and in his own way. Allow your little one some clinging time when you can. Respond to your baby's cry—even if he's fed, changed, and unhurt—even when his only need is to be held. Don't worry about spoiling him with your love and attention, since quite the opposite will happen. The more that you meet his attachment needs during early childhood, the more confident and secure he will grow up to be.

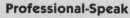

Professional-Speak

"There was an old theory that if you always picked up a child who was crying, then the child would learn to cry in order to get picked up, and the child would eventually cry more. We have found that exactly the opposite occurs: Children who are repeatedly, regularly, and consistently picked up and soothed when they cry end up crying less."

—**Penelope Leach, author of** *Your Baby & Child*

Minimize Separations When Possible

It's perfectly acceptable to avoid those situations that would have you separate from your child in the midst of a separation anxiety stage. Some people will try to convince you that it is important (maybe even *critically* important!) for you to force your child to deal with separations. The reality here is that no study has proven that a child who is forced to face this fear head-on will overcome it more easily or quickly than one who is allowed to adjust according to his own time frame. On the contrary, it makes far more sense to work with a child's needs to gently and lovingly nudge him toward the goal.

In situations where there is a choice and you don't feel compelled to make the separation, then don't. All too soon, your child will move past this phase and on to the next developmental milestone.

On the other hand, there are many days when the timing is right for separation, and your child is set up to be left in kind, capable

Key Point

There is no scientific proof that pushing a young child to separate from his mother, father, or other primary caregivers benefits his development. Quite the opposite is true: research tells us that healthy, strong attachments to primary caregivers in early childhood affect a child's behavior, development, and social relationships in very positive ways.

hands. When that is the case, use the gentle ideas presented throughout this book to help him adjust to periods of separation.

Let Your Child Enjoy Some Quiet "Alone Time" in the Crib or Bed

Many children wake up after a nap or in the morning and are content to look around the room, play with a toy, or daydream. Many parents are unaware that their child *can* do this, because the minute they hear a peep, they run to retrieve her. I suggest that you walk a little slower next time. Listen carefully to your child: Is she calling to you or fussing for attention? Or is she just waking up to her world and taking a few quiet minutes for herself? If she seems content, then keep an ear on her, but allow her this personal time.

Many parents believe that tending to a baby's needs—which you should always do—means that their baby can never be awake *and* alone. While having roots in good parenting philosophy, you need to know that a child *can* enjoy alone time to learn that she can be her own best company. Far from being neglectful, this is a lovely gift that you can give your child. This confidence can be a very handy tool that she can use to ward off feelings of separation anxiety in other situations.

Tell Your Child What to Expect

Even if you think your little one is too young to understand, get in the habit of telling him where you're going and when you'll be back. You don't have to tell him too far in advance—a baby or toddler won't understand or retain information about next weekend, for example. However, letting him know what to expect an hour or two before it happens, and then again as you are getting ready to leave is a good practice. "I'm going to the store soon. You'll be here with Grandma." Give him an idea of when you will return. Use an indicator he can understand, such as "I'll be back after lunch." Do this even with a preverbal baby, because eventually he will understand.

This same idea is useful if your child is going to be left somewhere, such as daycare, the church nursery, or the gym child-care center.

Chat about what's going to happen in the car or bus on the way to the event. That way your child will be prepared rather than surprised when he is left there without you.

Don't Sneak Away

Don't tiptoe away when your child is asleep or distracted. It may seem easier than dealing with a tearful good-bye, but it will just cause her constant worry that you're going to disappear without warning at any given moment in the future. The result can be even *more* clinginess, because she'll assume she must keep you in sight at all times. In addition, leaving when she is unaware of it can diminish her trust in you; she may interpret this as punishment or disrespect of her feelings.

Don't *Rush* the Parting

Give your baby ample time to process your leave-taking. A rushed period of chaos as you get ready to leave and then a mad dash out the door can easily set your child up for an episode of anxiety. Instead, create and use a short but pleasant good-bye ritual—certain words and actions you always use when you go. Be relaxed and cheerful. Allow ten or fifteen minutes for a proper, peaceful send-off.

Don't *Prolong* the Parting

While you want to allow your child sufficient time to accept that you are leaving, don't drag out the actual good-byes too long. Say, "Bye-bye," and leave with a wave and a smile. The longer you make the parting process, the more you allow your child's anxiety to grow. In addition, once you say good-bye, leave! Very often parents will be walking out the door, but then start a conversation with the caregiver or take a last-minute phone call. This creates confusion for your little one and can permit anxiety to creep in.

Once you say good-bye and your baby is settling down with the caregiver, don't come back in for any reason. Make sure you have your keys, tickets, purse, and coat in hand.

Express a Cheerful, Positive Attitude When Leaving

Children are very perceptive of their parents' feelings. Your baby will not only observe your actions, she will absorb your emotions. So if you're nervous about leaving her, she'll be nervous as well. Your confidence will help alleviate her fears and convey that she can handle this. When you show her that you are relaxed and confident, you're sending a message that she should relax as well.

This may not work at all the first time you do it. Or the second time. Maybe not even the third. But eventually your child will come to realize that you always happily say good-bye, nothing bad happens while you are gone, and you always come back, so there is nothing for her to worry about.

To convince your child that all is well, it is helpful if you really believe it! (See Chapter 6.)

Jan, nine months old

Have Practice Sessions: Leave Your Baby with Familiar People

To practice for upcoming separation, leave your child with a familiar, trusted, and loving person. Start with a short time, then make it progressively longer—ten minutes, twenty minutes, thirty minutes—until you reach an hour or two. For best results, do this every few days or at least twice a week, so that your baby remembers the experience from one time to the next.

When you are first having these practice situations, your baby might cry right after you leave. Try not to return while he is crying. You can hide at the door and wait until the caregiver is able to calm him. Since this is a person your baby trusts, she should be able to help your child stop crying. Prior to leaving, suggest the activities most likely to help, such as looking out the window, playing with the cat, or reading a book. When your baby settles down and is perhaps even playing happily with the sitter is the best time for you to return. If you show up during tears, your baby might think it's the tears that brought you back! If you return when your baby is happy, it will create a positive experience for his memory bank.

If possible, try to do this practice exercise for a few weeks or even a month or two before your child starts daycare or begins a new schedule with a babysitter.

If having a sitter is going to be a regular event, build up over time to your full daily stretch. It is helpful to pay for a few warm-up sessions first *while you remain at home*. Stay in the room the first few times, but as an uninvolved observer as much as possible. If your baby won't leave your side, then sit quietly but let the sitter talk and play with your child. Inch away as they become engaged.

After the first few fully attended sessions, allow the two of them to get involved in playtime or an activity, then leave the room and let them get to know each other. If you've already played the Bye-Bye game described earlier in this chapter, you should have no problem ducking out for a few minutes. You'll still be close, however, and can sing, hum, talk on the phone, or whistle if it helps. That way your child will feel your comforting presence in the house. If things are going well, then stay out of the room and keep very quiet. Let the sitter and your baby find their own rhythm together.

The next step in this process is to have the sitter over and leave the house for a short time, perhaps twenty minutes. If this goes well, leave for an hour or two. Then you'll be set for your full session. With the short sessions, your child will learn that you can leave, he'll be happy and safe with his caregiver, and you will return later. This pattern easily transfers to a longer time period.

When you return home, don't make it an emotional reunion; you'll just call his attention to the fact that the parting was a big deal. Give him a pleasant hello and a hug and then ask, "Did you have fun?" This lets your child know you are comfortable and confident with this new arrangement, and he should be too.

Cue the Caregiver's Helpful Response

It's a challenge for a caregiver to handle a child who cries as soon as a parent leaves. Many people are unsure what they should do, and most often, the instinctual response is a quietly murmured, "It's okay. Don't cry." This is usually accompanied with tight hugs and soothing rubs. This may work with some children, but with most, it tends to have little or no effect. The child's mind is filled with intense emotions, and reassuring words are drowned out by her own voice. In addition, the overly sympathetic actions convey to the child that the separation is, indeed, a very big deal.

Instead, suggest that your caregiver attempt to gain the child's attention with an active motion, such as cheerful hand clapping, and a distracting tone of voice that matches the volume and emotion of the child's response. Here, a more vigorous response, such as, "Wow! Wow! What's happening? Look at me! I'm here! I can help!" is in order. The caregiver's enthusiasm might be enough to turn the moment around.

Invite Distractions

Encourage your child's caregiver to get her involved with a toy or playtime as you leave. If your schedule permits, get them started while you are still there. Sit beside them for five minutes and introduce the toy or activity. Then move a few feet away and just watch them quietly. (Avoid any supportive comments that call attention to your presence.) Once they are engaged, say a quick good-bye and go.

By allowing your child to be distracted by an interesting toy, an activity, or a window-gazing conversation, your leaving becomes less of a focal point and gives the caregiver a tool to engage your child's attention.

Father-Speak

"Our neighbor is a mother of six, grandmother of ten, and great-grandmother of two. She's a peaceful woman, and her experience shows. Our daughter has extreme separation anxiety, but Abuelita (as everyone calls her) scoops her up and walks her through the garden, pointing out every leaf and bug with fascination in her voice. Daniela is so enthralled that she doesn't resist her like she does other people."

—Juan, father of one-year-old Daniela

Allow Your Baby the Separation That She Initiates

Often parents miss excellent opportunities to allow a baby to practice separation on her own agenda. These are the times during relaxed playtime when your child spies something new to investigate and moves off to explore. A natural response from a loving parent is to follow along and comment on the source of interest. This announces your presence and changes the child's private moment into a group activity—and misses a chance to allow the child to be her own company.

So if your little one crawls or toddles off to another room, don't rush after her! Peek to be sure she's safe, of course, but let her know it is fine to go off exploring on her own. You can set your child up for these self-initiated opportunities by placing new or favorite toys within sight but in another room or a short distance away from you.

A child-initiated separation is a brilliant time to allow your little one to experience what a happy separation feels like. Let your baby have these short, independent play sessions every day. If your baby is happily playing alone or quietly taking in his surroundings, keep your distance, enjoy the view, and let him absorb the fact that he *can* be alone and still be safe and happy. This practice will help him deal with future separations over which he won't have control. In addition, being able to play alone is a valuable life skill that will boost your child's self-confidence and inner peace.

Encourage Your Child's Relationship with a Lovey

A preferred toy, blanket, or stuffed animal is called a "transitional object," because it is a tool for the transition between being with a parent and being alone. It is a familiar object that gives a child reassurance that everything is normal. The common (and accurate) terms for a transitional object are *security blanket* or *lovey* because children develop very strong emotional ties to these items. A lovey can be a comfort to your child and ease the pain of separation. The lovey becomes a friend and represents security.

Many children gravitate to a particular blanket or toy on their own. If you notice this in your child, celebrate this special relationship and respect it. If your child doesn't have a lovey, you can make an effort to encourage her. Choose a blanket or stuffed animal that you think may be a candidate, perhaps something she often touches or carries. (Mommy's old T-shirt can make a great lovey for a clingy baby.) Choose a lovey wisely if you have a say in the matter, because it may be around for years to come.

Once you've chosen a possibility, keep the item around often, particularly at bedtime, naptime, and cuddle time. Eventually your child will gravitate to this special toy or blanket. Then you can rely on it to help your child during separations.

A word of caution: If your child develops an attachment to a lovey, make your best effort to own two or three of them. Rotate them so that one doesn't become more worn than the others. (The wear and tear is part of the lovey's personality.) There is no disaster as great as a lost or damaged lovey!

Introduce People Gently

When introducing your baby to new people, hold her securely in your arms. The safety of your embrace will help her feel more comfortable with the unknown. Don't force her to be held or touched by

Grandpa ("Baba") David and Malky, twenty-two months old

others if she is not comfortable. This might even *increase* her fear the next time she faces a close encounter with a stranger. Wait until she warms up to the person visually before encouraging a physical connection.

This is also the first lesson in teaching your baby how to protect herself and her personal space. You do this by showing her that you respect her wishes and by giving her permission to make choices in situations regarding her own body.

Understand That People Familiar to You May Be Strangers to Your Baby

Although you may be very familiar with aunts, uncles, grandparents, or friends, if your baby hasn't seen much of these people, he will categorize them as "strangers." This isn't a judgment of your family members—just an indication that your baby doesn't know them well. The toughest challenge is helping these people understand that time and patience are necessary to help him become more comfortable with them.

To help your baby accept new people, it's helpful to keep him in your arms as you talk to them. You may want to reach out and hug them or touch them in a loving way to show your baby that you accept them as friends, and it's okay for him to do the same.

Provide information to reduce the "stranger's" feeling of offense. A simple explanation is a good way to take the edge off the situation. Say something like, "It takes him a few minutes to warm up to someone he doesn't know well. I read that this is normal for his age." This removes the discomfort felt by anyone when a child reacts as if that person is a threat to his very existence! Once you've made this brief statement, launch into an unrelated topic of conversation. This gives

Key Point

Any person your child does not know well is a stranger to him.

your child a chance to regroup and watch this new person without being the center of attention.

Let Your Baby Set the Pace

Encourage a new person to "ignore" your baby and wait for the baby to come to her. Explain in advance that your child is in the throes of separation anxiety and you've discovered that letting her initiate contact helps get things off on the right foot. Doing this can set the pace for interaction, since the new person won't take your baby's cold shoulder personally.

After allowing your little one some time to observe the newcomer, give the guest a toy to share with your child. A nice person holding an interesting toy is easier to accept than one reaching out to hold or touch your baby. Children are naturally curious, and this strategy takes the focus off the stress of meeting a new person and instead places it on the neutral or familiar plaything.

Your child will feel some control over the situation if she's not pushed and will be more likely to respond in positive ways to this visit and in the future when she meets her next new friend.

Let Your Baby Safely Observe More New People

The more your baby is around new people, the more comfortable he'll be with new faces. Expose your child to groups of people in places where he can observe without the pressure to interact with them. Take walks around the mall or go to a busy park. Keep your baby close, and let him look around and absorb his world and all the new faces in it.

Your child will look to you for cues that people are safe to relate to, so be cheerful with cashiers, salespeople, or others you come across. If one of these strangers talks to your baby, you can jump in and answer on his behalf. If they attempt to reach out to touch or hold him, you can swiftly interject that he's "a little shy," which is a universally accepted reason for his hesitance.

Rescue Your Baby as Soon as She Needs You

Separation anxiety doesn't disappear fully in one day; it usually happens in fits and starts over a period of time. Your baby might accept being held by someone, but minutes later decide it's too much for her. If she begins to look stressed or starts to cry, then go ahead scoop her back up immediately (if you can). You don't need to passively watch someone trying to calm your crying baby. A brief explanation helps ease the discomfort of the situation: "Oops. She still has some separation anxiety, and it looks like it just kicked in." Most people will be relieved that you took care of your crying baby so quickly.

If your baby is pushed beyond her comfort level, she may tighten up her reins on you and resist the next attempt. Allowing her a rescue when she calls for it means she'll be willing to try again. Short, pleasant experiences will naturally grow into longer ones.

Preintroduce Your Baby to New People

To prepare your baby for upcoming times with unfamiliar people, show her home movies and photos the week before the visit. If your child likes books, then make a homemade book of photos to share with her as you talk about these lovely people.

When they finally arrive in person, *you* should hug and greet them first and call them by name, so your baby can make the connection between the photos and the actual people.

Eat, Drink, Rest, and Be Merry

A child who is well rested will make new friends or adapt to a parting from Mom or Dad much easier than a tired one. Tired children have shorter fuses—you can take their normal comfort zone and divide that in half!

A hungry child can also be too uncomfortable to adapt. Children cannot always identify their discomfort as hunger, and when they are out of sorts they naturally gravitate toward the person who knows them best and who can alleviate their discomfort.

Alyssa, two years old, and Matthew, four years old

A baby who is well rested and not feeling hungry will be in a better mood to socialize or explore new situations.

Avoid Excess Separation During Peak Anxiety Phases

It is perfectly okay to avoid separating from your child during peaks in separation anxiety, since these phases usually pass more quickly if allowed to follow a more relaxed path. It's also not the time to schedule a prolonged absence from your child, such as a daylong shopping trip, a lengthy session at the health club daycare center, or an overnight at a relative's home.

If you need to separate from your child during peak times of anxiety, choose the babysitter carefully. Beyond the basics of someone who is capable of giving good care, look for someone who is sympathetic to your child's anxiety and will respond with gentleness and patience.

Yet don't take avoidance to the extreme and become hermits because your baby is nervous about new situations or meeting new people! Instead, take it slow and easy, and you can help your child grow out of this stage sooner and easier.

Monitor Your Responses

If you are nervous about leaving your baby, she will pick up on your feelings. She'll take cues about how to act directly from you. Show your confidence: your baby will be in good care while you are apart and will likely have fun once she adjusts to your departure. So stay calm, confident, and relaxed so you can pass these emotions on to your child.

Downplay your return as well. If your baby struggled while you were away and then you return to cover her head with kisses and tell her how much you missed her, you inadvertently send the message that separation is, indeed, a big deal and something to be feared. Instead, greet her with a hug and a friendly yet calm reunion. Keep your voice cheerful: "Hi, sweetie! Did you play with your new blocks while I was gone?" This tells her that the separation is normal, the reunion with you is ordinary life, and the parting was nothing to worry about.

Build on Good Experiences

If you have a successful separation event, try to re-create it within a few days. Don't wait too long, as the optimistic mood is best kept alive if you act quickly. A growing store of positive experiences will build your child's confidence.

3

The Magic Bracelet Solution for No-Cry Separation

What is the only thing that would completely eliminate separation anxiety? Eliminating the separation, of course! If your child could take *you* along wherever he went, then all would be well. Since that is clearly impossible, you can do the next best thing—provide your child with a memento that gives him a feeling of security and is a visible token of your love when you are apart. I've discovered that an easy-to-wear, accessible memento that works for boys and girls of all ages is the Magic Bracelet. Think of the bracelet as a portable you—albeit a you that is squashed, flattened, and worn around your child's wrist.

In the same way that a well-loved blanket or a stuffed animal lovey is a transitional object to help your child feel secure when leaving you at bedtime, the Magic Bracelet is a transitional object to help him separate from you with confidence during the day (and can be used as a sleep-time aid as well). It is a tangible reminder of your love and care that can be worn easily all day long, may be touched or viewed whenever necessary, and carries with it a portable and easily accessible sign of comfort and affection.

Let's look at how one mother, Christine, used the Magic Bracelet to help her son. She first e-mailed me with this plea:

Dear Elizabeth,

I'm writing because of my six-year-old son, Lucas. He just started kindergarten and is having great difficulty separating from me. He misses me too much, and he doesn't want to go to school. He cries every morning at home and then cries when I drop him off at school. It breaks my heart to walk away when he is in such a state, and it starts the day off on such a horrible note for both of us.

When I pick Lucas up from school, he seems okay and says he had fun. The teacher tells me that he settles in and functions well during the school day. However, by bedtime he is anxious and worried about school again. He isn't sleeping well, and he barely eats breakfast or his lunch on school days. . . . I know it's because he's nervous.

Is this normal behavior? Is there anything I can do to help him? I have spoken to his teacher. She says it's not uncommon and to give it time. Yet it's so difficult to leave him in such a state every morning. I worry about Lucas all day long.

I would appreciate any advice you could offer me. I'm having a hard enough time with the adjustment of him going off to kindergarten, but add his crying and pleading into the mix and I feel absolutely terrible. :(

Thank you for your time. I hope to hear back from you soon!

Sincerely,
Christine, mother of six-year-old Lucas and four-year-old Levi

I wish I could have hugged Christine and her little Lucas right then and there! I could feel her pain, because I've lived through it before, and I also understood her little boy's uncertainty and fear. I could imagine the stress and frustration their mornings held.

I wrote back to Christine and assured her that Lucas was very normal. Making the move to kindergarten is a big step in a child's life (see Chapter 4). I gave her hope that we could work it through. I sent her some information and a whole list of tips and gave her instructions on how to create and use a Magic Bracelet. Her next note arrived an astonishingly short six days later:

Hi, Elizabeth!

Thank you! Thank you! Thank you! Thank you! :)

I followed all your ideas this week, and I made a bracelet for Lucas immediately after receiving your e-mail. I gave it to him the next morning, explaining that it carried my love in it. I held it to my heart, gave it hugs and kisses, and told him that anytime he felt sad or missed me, all he had to do was touch the bracelet and he would feel my love.

His face brightened up! It was like the key to peace for him. He really liked this idea, and off he went to school—actually smiling!

We are now five school days, absolutely, wonderfully, 100 percent tear-free! :O

He asks me every morning to "put my love" into the bracelet and happily puts it on. Today, as we were leaving for school, he said, "Thank you, Mama, for making me this bracelet. It helps me a lot." I was speechless.

I can't begin to tell you how much this has changed our home. Thank you sooo very much!

My four-year-old son, Levi, just started preschool, so I made one for him too. He was doing okay (anything is okay compared to Lucas's problems), but the bracelet has made our mornings with Levi much easier too.

I have spoken with several other parents at school who are having separation issues as well and have told them your advice and the results we've seen. There will probably be a few more preschoolers and kindergartners walking around school with Magic Bracelets next week.

You have my sincere and heartfelt thanks, and I am sure Lucas's thanks as well.

Fondly,
Christine

Your Child's Magic Bracelet

The first step to putting this idea into practice is to find the perfect bracelet for your child. I've gotten you started by including a special gift with this book—a bracelet already infused with magic and ready to use. This bracelet may work perfectly for your child and might be all you need, but for any number of reasons, you might decide to choose a bracelet of your own. The actual bracelet is not what's important—it is the power it holds.

If you discover that a Magic Bracelet becomes a cherished part of your little one's separation confidence, you'll want to have one or two more as backups in case the original bracelet is lost or damaged, as is common with young children's belongings. Should you use the bracelet included here, you can visit my website at www.nocrysolution.com to order more.

As an alternative, you can buy or make your own bracelet for your child. If you do, make sure the bracelet fits the following criteria:

- It has no small parts that could be potential choking hazards for your child or younger friends or siblings.
- It is sturdy enough to stand up to playtime and heavy use.
- It is easy for your child to put on and take off.
- It is a simple, unobtrusive style that can be worn for the next year or longer, if necessary.
- It is easy to replace if lost or broken.

Once you have a second backup bracelet, I suggest that you rotate the two bracelets frequently. If you keep one tucked away, and your child wears the other every day, it may become tattered or defaced in some way that makes it unique and thus absolutely irreplaceable in your child's eyes. Keep the second bracelet safely hidden so your child doesn't find it and misplace it or develop a bond to wearing *two* bracelets at the same time.

Daddy David and twins Ava and Julian, seventeen months old

Introduce Your Child to the Magic Bracelet

It is critically important for you to introduce the bracelet properly to your child. This is not something to be thrust into her hands at a time when she is crying frantically and watching you walk away, even if you're tempted to do so. Such a beginning would likely create negative feelings about the bracelet and prevent any future positive use. You will need to infuse the bracelet with loving "magic" before your child walks off with it happily on her wrist.

Introduce the bracelet idea gently, lovingly, and in a relaxed manner. Even though you might have to live through another few days of separation anxiety tears, it is better to take the time to warm your child up to the idea than to rush it or present it at the wrong time and destroy the opportunity to use this tremendously helpful tool.

Introduce the bracelet on a day when both you and your child are in a good mood and you are feeling connected. You may wish to wrap it up and present it as a special gift.

Depending on your child's personality and your own opinion about things like the Easter bunny, Santa Claus, and the tooth fairy, you can either give the bracelet a "magic" quality or simply present it as a confidence-building tool to make parting easier. Here are scripts that show how two different parents explained the gift to their children:

The Truly Magic Bracelet

"Mommy has something very special here. This is a magic bracelet I got especially for you. It will help you feel better every day when you go to daycare. It will be almost like having a tiny, little Mommy to take with you! It can carry hugs and kisses and love, so anytime you need some love from me, you will have it right there on your wrist. You just have to look at it or touch it, and it will make you feel better. Would you like to try it on?" (Parent places the bracelet carefully and lovingly on the child's wrist, and then hugs it and kisses it and places the child's arm with the bracelet up to her chest to give it a final hug.)

The Confidence-Builder Bracelet

"I know that it's hard for you to leave me in the morning when you go to school. So I have something very special for you that I think will help you a lot. It's called a Magic Bracelet because it helps kids feel better when they are away from home. I love you all the time—even when we are not together—and your bracelet with help you remember that I am loving you even when I am not with you. You just have to look at it or touch it, and it can make you feel better. Would you like to try it on?" (Parent gives the bracelet a hug and a kiss, and then places it gently and lovingly on the child's wrist.)

More Tips for Introducing the Bracelet Idea

Every child is unique, and you know your little one best. Either of these two scripts might be perfect for you, or you may need to lead up to the moment and prepare your child for the actual presentation. Here are a series of ideas that have worked for other parents when beginning work with the Magic Bracelet. Take some time to review them, think about what might work best for you, and set up a plan before you begin.

First Mine, Now Yours

Children who are intent on mimicking everything a parent does might take to the bracelet if they first see it as something that Mommy or Daddy wears. In this case, *you* will wear the bracelet all day for several days, keeping it highly visible to your child, until he associates it with you. Once it's a familiar piece of you, then you can offer

---

Mother-Speak

"Gracie loves anything that is mine. She'll wear my scarves, my shoes, and my jewelry, and she carries my purse around the house. Keeping this in mind, I wore the bracelet myself over the weekend, making sure to keep it so Gracie could see it. When I finally offered it to her on Monday morning, she was ecstatic! Because it was mine, she treated it like gold. It's become a perfect charm to calm her in the morning."

—Erika, mother of four-year-old Grace

to let him wear it when he's away from home. Because it is "yours" and your child has seen it as part of you, it can bring a strong feeling of home and safety. If you wear cologne every day, then you can spritz the bracelet with a bit of your scent each morning to remind your child of you.

A Bearer of Good Feelings

For some children, it can help to first create a good feeling surrounding the times when the bracelet is worn. In this case, you will give your child the bracelet at a happy time. This might be on a day at home when you have extra time for play, or it could be on a special family outing, like a day at the park. You can first incorporate it into your quiet reading and cuddling times before using it when your child ventures away from home. Once the bracelet carries memories of safe, happy family times, it can be a comfort when used away from home.

How to Use the Magic Bracelet

Keep your child's Magic Bracelet in a safe, specific place, so it will be there when you need it. You might install a special hook or shelf near the door so the bracelet can be taken off when your child arrives home and easily retrieved as you leave.

If you drive your child to and from school, you may want to keep the bracelet in a special place in the car. Putting it on and taking it off can be part of the ritual of parting and reuniting each day.

It can help to have a routine for donning the bracelet. You might always put it on your child and then give it a hug and kiss, saying some "magic" words in the process.

Magic Words

Whether you impart your child's bracelet with magic powers or simply provide it as a token to build confidence, I suggest coming up with a phrase that you say at the time you put it on her wrist. These words become part of the ritual and are one more significant element of the enchantment.

Father-Speak

"The first time I put the bracelet on Emerson's wrist, I waved my pen over it like a magic wand and said some fancy mumbo-jumbo magic words. Now I have to wave the pen and do the magic words every time!"

—**Tim, father of five-year-old Emerson**

Your Magic Bracelet phrase should be something short and sweet, as over time it may become something to be whispered quickly in her ear when the two of you part. Often this phrase is used for a long time, even after the bracelet is set aside in a drawer and a touch to the wrist is all that is needed to bring back all the calming feelings.

The magic words are something you can say to your child or something you can recite together. Here are some examples of other parents' magic words that you can use as ideas to create your own phrase:

"Here are lots of tiny little mommy hugs to keep with you all day long. Have a great day!"

"Remember, your Magic Bracelet is like having Mama at school with you. Just touch it whenever you need a hug!"

"Magic bracelet just for you.
Hugs and kisses in it too.
Wear it all day with a smile,
'Cuz Daddy loves you all the while."

The Magic Bracelet Put-Away Routine

It's a good idea to create a routine for taking off the bracelet and putting it away when your child arrives home so that it is clearly for use when you are apart. A bracelet worn all day will lose its "separation" value and is more easily misplaced. There is nothing worse than discovering a bracelet is lost just as you are heading out the door to leave for daycare or school! (Should that happen, though, this is where your backup bracelet comes into play. Keep an extra one in a hidden, safe place for this purpose.)

Once your child is dependent on his bracelet to get him through the day, it will be an important token, and a day without a bracelet can get off to a rocky start. Be prepared to deliver a forgotten bracelet to daycare or school.

When to Use the Magic Bracelet

The Magic Bracelet can be used anytime you and your child are apart, whether he does the leaving or you do. A few examples of times when the bracelet can be a successful tool:

- Daycare
- School
- Babysitting event
- Child care at the health club, shopping mall, or church
- Hospital stay
- Camp
- Vacation
- Birthday parties
- Playdates
- Sleepovers
- Family visits
- Business trips
- Divorced parents/two homes
- Naptime
- Nighttime sleep

Weaning Your Child from the Magic Bracelet

Children draw on the power of their bracelets in different ways, and they all lose their need for it in different ways too. It's rarely a one-day event. Usually there is a gradual reduction of its importance. Because the bracelet is inconspicuous and easy to wear, there is no need to persuade your child to stop wearing it. If you can, allow the association to progress on its own and to fade on your child's own unique time line.

You will likely notice that the bracelet becomes less significant to your child over time. She may "forget" to ask for it or tell you that

Jessica, three years old, and Mommy Sharrie

she doesn't need it on a particular morning. If that happens, you may want to put it into your child's backpack so she can carry it along with her but no longer wear it on her wrist. That way if she changes her mind, hits a difficult moment, or suddenly remembers she forgot to wear it after you've parted, she'll still have access to it.

Once the bracelet is left behind more than it's worn, or when it settles permanently into the bottom of the backpack without being used, you'll know that your child has grown past the need to use its magic. Even after that happens, though, keep the bracelet in a safe place so it can be reintroduced in times of need. It's possible that your child will face separation issues in the future, such as a first overnight visit, a hospital stay, or a particularly difficult transition. If the bracelet worked once, it is very likely to work again if the need arises. If not, it will be a wonderful keepsake to allow you both to remember and cherish your child's growth and maturity.

4

No-Cry Solutions for Preschool and School-Age Children

As children move past babyhood, their world expands. They find themselves in situations that take them further away from the familiarity of home and parents. This can be a challenge for a child whose budding independence beckons him away but whose lack of experience and confidence draws him back home. Children's independence develops in bursts, which are frequently interspersed with regression back to safer territory. A normal maturity process is not a straight arrow; it's more a wavy line that gradually makes its way along stepping-stones of separation anxiety all the way to adulthood.

Every child is unique, so the right combination of ideas for thwarting separation anxiety is different for each one. The Magic Bracelet is an idea that can help many children with their separation anxiety. However, some may need more than just the bracelet, and some may have a rough start and need additional ideas to help them during the transition period. This section will provide you with an assortment of ideas that can be used along with the Magic Bracelet or by themselves.

You know your child best, so once you read through all the suggestions, you will be able to put together a good plan for your little one. Don't worry if things aren't perfect from the get-go. Just revisit the solutions and revise your plan. In time you will hit on the right combination of solutions to help your child feel good about moving away from you and heading out into the big, wide world with confidence.

Play Separation Games

You can reduce the stress of separation by making it less intimidating through casual practice. You can achieve this goal by playing games that include separation. A good game to play is hide-and-seek, which you can play in the house or at the park or playground. Another option is to have a treasure hunt, where your child follows clues around the house or yard to find a surprise at the end. Make the game even more fun by hiding small tokens along the way. To enhance the separation aspect of this game, you should stay in one place, such as the kitchen, while your child wanders around and hunts. He can ring a bell (or yell "Yahoo!") when a treasure is found, and you can respond with a shout of encouragement.

Tell Your Child What to Expect

When you give your child specific information about upcoming times of separation, you can eliminate fears that are based on speculation and fueled by imagination. If you are going to the store, for example, and leaving her at home with Grandma, explain where you are going, what she'll do while you're gone, and when you'll be back.

When you give advance notice, describe in detail what to expect. Children who have separation anxiety are often fearful of the unknown. If separations happen without warning or if things are not as expected, they begin looking over their shoulder for the next unexpected event. So help your child out by giving her specific details.

Children love to anticipate positive events, so if a separation situation is coming up, talk about the imminent event in a relaxed and encouraging way. You don't want to start too early, but based on your child's age and the scope of the event, you might begin talking about it a few days or a week in advance.

Chat with your child about what will happen, but spread this out over various short conversations. It's helpful if you come from a position of emotional strength: assume your child will be fine while she's away from you. Avoid talking about her fears or concerns, unless she brings them up. If she does, acknowledge these feelings without giving them too much power. Move on again to the specific details of the event. This process can help prepare your child by giving her a more concrete picture in her mind of what to expect.

Promise to Return, and Then Remind Your Child of the Promise

When you leave, your child will be wondering when you will be back. You don't want him to guess, as this can add to his worry. A brief statement about your reunion can be very helpful. Try to tie your return to an event, rather than a time on the clock, for two reasons. First, giving a specific time can backfire if you are a bit late; a general time period is more flexible. Second, cueing your return to an event gives predictability to your child's day; for example, "I'll be home after you wake up from your nap," or "I'll be outside waiting when the school bell rings."

When you are reunited, remind him that you are there when you promised: "See? I came home after your nap, just like I said." This reminder builds confidence for your next separation.

When your child is in the midst of bouts of separation anxiety, work hard not to be late—even by a few minutes. If you are running late, make sure you call and get a message to your child that you are on the way. This reassures him that you will soon be there.

Understand the Age-Appropriateness of the Anxiety

Separation anxiety is a normal and biologically necessary emotion. It's a sign of your child's deep love and attachment to you. It isn't something your child can control by himself, and it isn't something he is doing to annoy you. It is a phase that children outgrow over time, and it is a process that can be moved along when you take active steps to help your child.

Children with separation anxiety can't explain their feelings, but they know those feelings are not good. Their uncertainty can present itself in many ways that may resemble misbehavior to an unknowing

Professional-Speak

"Anxiety in kids can look sometimes like defiance, rebellion, anger, or stubbornness, when it's really kids panicking because they are so afraid."

—Mark Crawford, M.D., clinical psychologist

adult. A child who is fussy, inflexible, or having a whale of a tantrum may inadvertently push away the adult he is trying so hard to attach to.

Allow Your Child to Warm Up to New Situations

Throwing a child headfirst into a situation he's nervous about is akin to tossing him in the water to teach him to swim. Don't force your child to go far beyond his comfort zone. Instead, permit him to observe the situation, learn more about it, and approach it a bit at a time, whenever possible. Allow him to watch from the sidelines for a while to absorb the goings-on and get a feel for how he'll fit into the picture. Let him know he can sit and watch for as long as he wants to before joining in, since this takes the pressure off. Many children relax when they know they have permission to take their time getting involved. Once a child is relaxed, he'll be more willing to extend himself.

Introduce New People Gradually

When introducing your child to a new person, hold her hand or put your arm around her. Require no more than a hello. It's not a time to demand that your child converse with this new person or answer complex questions. If the newcomer talks to your obviously suffering child, it's perfectly okay to answer for her so she can warm up before fully participating in the conversation. The safety of your touch and lack of pressure to have a full conversation will help her feel more comfortable and build her confidence.

Tell Stories That Teach

Some children will relax more if you explain an upcoming event in an indirect way that takes the spotlight off their own participation and helps them examine the situation from an outsider's point of view. Do this by telling your child a story using familiar characters that he likes, putting them into the situation that he'll be facing. SpongeBob can go to visit his aunt and spend the night at her house, for example. This permits you to warm your child up to the situation and explore it from someone else's experience before he has to face it himself. Do this several times over a week or two prior to your child's actual event, so that by the time it's his turn, it will feel more familiar.

Have a Dress Rehearsal

Children who have healthy imaginations and like to play make-believe games have a built-in method to prepare them for upcoming events. Several times in advance of a new situation you can play a

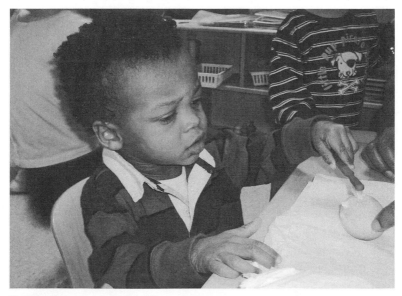

Keliah, sixteen months old

game where you mimic what will happen. For example, if your child is going to be spending the night with a babysitter, you can dress up as the sitter (put on a hat, scarf, and sunglasses). Playact the upcoming situation, making it fun and being cheerful all the while. Try to make the details realistic (ring the doorbell, walk in, say hello, review the events of the evening, then say good-bye to the imaginary mom and dad). Once the make-believe parents are gone, go through some of the actions that might occur. For example, in your role as babysitter, play a game and make a snack using items you'll then actually provide to the real sitter.

Create Baby Steps of Autonomy

Rather than focusing on a full-blown situation of long-term separation, provide opportunities for your child to take small steps toward independence. For example, take your child to a familiar park, and once he's involved in an activity, move a short distance away, sit on a bench, and read a book. Every once in a while, touch base with him, if necessary, by waving or making a comment such as, "Wow! You're swinging high." However, if he doesn't look to you for this reassurance, then avoid offering it, since you want to support his ability to be confident when he's away from you.

Give Your Child a Calming Trinket

An anxious child can sometimes be calmed by having something to stroke or squeeze, thereby releasing some of his nervous energy. Give your child a tiny stuffed animal or a lucky charm, like a squishy ball. You might give him something of yours, like an old key chain or a soft scarf. Before separating, give the charm a kiss and hug and put it in your child's pocket. Explain that he can hold on to it whenever he wants and feel the love there. This is a similar idea to that of a Magic Bracelet (described in Chapter 3) but uses a slightly different type of item in a somewhat different way.

Visit in Advance

If your child is to be left at school, daycare, or a sitter's home, visit a few days beforehand just to check it out. Introduce her to the teachers, show her the cubbies, and play with the toys. While you are there, make an effort to avoid being a constant presence—step back from time to time so your child can feel what it will be like without you there. Talk about the experience later at home and mention what a great job she did; bring up some of the highlights and interesting things she saw. Tell her that you're confident she'll have fun when she's there next.

Have a Specific Routine for Parting

If your child will be spending time at daycare, school, or elsewhere on a regular basis, then have a very specific routine for the events leading up to separation. You can even make a poster with your morning routine described in detail. The steps can be demonstrated with drawings or photos. Follow your chart every day, exactly the same way, to build the routine into a comfortable rhythm.

It can help to create a secret handshake, a good-bye phrase, or other key components of leave-taking that you follow each time to create a bonding ritual before parting. This can give your child closure about your separation. In addition, the familiar sequence of

---

Mother-Speak

"Logan has a special way to say good-bye to me every morning when I leave for work. He carries my keys to the door, and then he finds my shoes. I put them on and take the keys and thank him for his help. Then we have a big squeeze, a tickle, and some kisses. If I leave out any of these things, he can't seem to get on with his day."

—Laura, mother of three-year-old Logan

events reassures her that what is happening is normal and reminds her that you will be together again soon.

Don't Plant Worry Seeds

In our effort to reassure our children we sometimes inadvertently increase their concerns. Saying things like, "Don't worry," "I'll be right here if you need me," or "Everything is going to be okay" aren't as reassuring as you might think. For many children, your concern about their worry actually implies that they really do have something to worry about. And placing a thought about the need to call you for help can raise a red flag in your child's mind: *Will I worry? Will I need to call for help?*

Instead of planting these worry seeds, make your comments positive in nature and get the message across that what he's about to do is no big deal—it's even fun. For example, when he's leaving your side to attend a birthday party, let him leave on a positive note with a cheerful good-bye and a mention of the good time he's about to have: "Have fun with the piñata! You can tell me about it when I pick you up."

Have a Specific Routine for Your Reunion

A reunion routine builds security and muscle memory for your child's thought processes. Do and say the same exact things every time you reunite—use the same phrase, make up a special "greeting handshake" or a special kind of hug. You might bring a small snack that your child can look forward to each day (if the timing is appropriate). Give your child 100 percent of your attention and eye-to-eye contact during pickup so that the reunion is something lovely she looks forward to.

Key Point

Children find sanctuary in specific routines that are built around the focal points of their day: morning rituals, mealtime, drop-offs, pickups, and bedtime.

Read Children's Books About Similar Situations

There are many books about children going to daycare, preschool, and kindergarten or staying with babysitters and about parents going off to work or on a trip. These books allow your child to glimpse the situation she'll be facing in a relaxed and less personal way. Children who enjoy books can learn many things from characters who do the same things they do. Read these books yourself first to be sure they fit your needs, then share them with your child to familiarize her with what to expect.

Give Your Child a Photo of You

Many children are comforted by a photo of their parents or siblings to view whenever they are feeling unsettled. The photo can act as a reminder of home and security. A picture or two placed in a small wallet or a locket can give your child a piece of you to have with her whenever you are apart.

Send a Funny Face Along with Your Child

If your child is reluctant to part from you, use a permanent marker to draw a happy face on your child's hand. Give it hair like yours and glasses if you wear them. Tell your child it's like having a mini-Mommy or tiny Daddy with him all day long. Most children are so impressed that you actually drew on their hand that the laughter that accompanies the drawing makes it extra special.

Acknowledge His Feelings

Let your child know that it's normal to be a little sad when you miss someone, but even with those sad feelings inside, he can still have fun. Acknowledging his feelings will help him begin to understand and accept them.

Johnathan, fifteen months old

Once you've acknowledged his emotions, take the next step: reassure him that he can deal with those feelings and learn to compartmentalize them alongside other more peaceful emotions and get on with the business of having fun. This process is important because it lets your child know that he is normal, which can be a relief since he may feel he's the only one who feels anxious. After this reassurance, turn your child's attention away from his concerns and toward a productive activity.

Here are a few reassuring comments that test parents reported using with their children:

> "I can see you're a little nervous about joining the party. That's okay, lots of kids are nervous when there are new people to meet. Let's see who you know. . . . Look, there's Trenton. Why don't you go over and show him your new watch?"

> "I know it's hard to leave Mommy for the day. That's because we love each other and we like to be together. Just like last week, you'll do lots of fun things at daycare, then I'll be here when you get home, and you can tell me about your day."

Don't let your child's uneasiness turn into full-blown fear. He may be unsure of a new place or person—that's normal. But in an effort to

Professional-Speak

"Physiological factors such as sleep, stimulation, and food affect the anxiety response. Any child will be more easily agitated if she has not had enough sleep or has ingested too many candy bars or sugary, caffeinated soft drinks."

—**John S. Dacey, Ph.D., and Lisa B. Fiore, Ph.D., authors of**
Your Anxious Child: How Parents and Teachers Can Relieve Anxiety in Children

help him relax, you might inadvertently increase his apprehension. Avoid saying things like, "There is nothing to be afraid of," or "Why are you scared?" since fear may not be the emotion he's feeling, and your words may create that option. Instead, make more general comments such as, "It's okay if you're not sure about this. It's something new. I bet you'll have lots of fun!"

Watch Your Child's Sleep Schedule and Eating Habits

Children who are tired, hungry, or nutritionally shortchanged have compromised biological systems from which to function. Their emotions are more volatile, which means they can suffer from more separation anxiety.

A child's daily diet should give him the proper fuel to keep his blood sugar and energy levels stable and provide him with the nutrients to keep his body and mind functioning properly.

Make sure your child gets enough sleep every night and appropriate daily naps. The actual number of hours he sleeps is an incredibly important factor for his health and well-being. Even a *one-hour* shortage in appropriate sleep time will compromise a child's brain function, increase fatigue, and make him more prone to negative emotions such as anxiety.

In addition to overall hours slept, the length of time your child is awake from one sleep period to the next will have an impact on his mood and behavior. When children are pushed beyond their biological awake time span without a break, they become fatigued, fussy, and unhappy. They cling more to their parents to gain a feeling of security.

As a child progresses through his day, his biology demands a sleep break to regroup. If he does not get this break, the problem intensifies: the rumblings and tremors become an outright explosion. The scientific term for this process is "homeostatic sleep pressure"; I call it the "volcano effect," as it is often as clear as watching a volcano erupt. Without a nap break, this pressure builds, growing in intensity—like a volcano—so that a child becomes tired and unable to stop the explosion. The result is a child who displays more intense emotions of all types, including separation anxiety.

The following chart is an important guide to your child's sleep hours. All children are different, and a few truly do need less (or more) sleep than shown here, but the vast majority of children have needs that fall within these ranges.

Sleep Chart: Average Hours of Daytime and Nighttime Sleep and Awake Periods*

Age	Number of Naps	Total Hours of Naptime	Endurable Awake Hours	Total Hours of Night Sleep*	Total Hours of Sleep per Day**
6 months	2–3	3–4	2–3	10–11	14–15
9 months	2	2½–4	2–4	11–12	14
1 year	1–2	2–3	3–4	11½–12	13½–14
2 years	1	1½–3	5–6½	11–12	13–13½
3 years	1	1–2	6–8	11–11½	12–13
4 years	0–1	0–2	6–12	11–11½	11½–12½
5 years	0–1	0–2	6–12	11	11–12
6 years	0–1	0–2	6–13	10½–11	10–11

*These are averages that do not necessarily represent *unbroken* stretches of sleep, since a brief awakening between sleep cycles is normal.
**The total hours shown for naps and nighttime sleep don't always add up, because when children take longer naps, they may sleep less at night and vice versa.

The No-Cry Separation Anxiety Solution © Better Beginnings, Inc.

Making Bedtime Separation Easier

Reduce bedtime separation anxiety with a very specific bedtime routine. Make a chart with the steps illustrated, using photos, drawings, or pictures from magazines. Follow the chart every night—right down to "lights out," "close eyes," and "sleep." Make it a relaxing, unrushed process. If the routine is predictable, your child will learn to accept it.

Reduce middle-of-the-night separation anxiety by having a specific night-waking routine. If you *sometimes* let your child come into your bed, *sometimes* stay with him in his bed, and *sometimes* require him to sleep alone, you'll be adding stress and confusion to his anxiety. Have a very specific night-waking plan and follow it every time. For more solutions about sleep-related separation anxiety, see Chapter 5.

Provide Ample "Chill Time"

A child who is rushed between daycare or school, errands, and other activities will tend to be more anxious overall. To help your child maintain an inner peace, build "chill time"—when he does "nothing"—into every day. Relaxed playtime is very productive and beneficial. It can help a child develop an inner quietness, much like yoga or meditation for an adult. A child with more inner peace will be less likely to succumb to anxious emotions.

Mother-Speak

"Thanks for the reminder to build some downtime into our day. I realized that I've been so busy rushing from place to place to place to place that my youngest was lost in the shuffle. No wonder he wouldn't let go of me when he finally had a hold of me!"

—Rachel, mother of eight-year-old Kate, six-year-old Grayson, and three-year-old Oliver

Arrange Regular Playdates with Special Friends

Children who must spend days in daycare or school will suffer less homesickness if they have familiar friends to connect with. Set up an at-home playtime with one or two daycare or school friends. Having someone from school who also comes to your home will create a link between the two places.

Key Point
Friendships with other children ease the pain of separation from Mom and Dad.

Have a Relaxed Morning Routine

If your child struggles with leaving for daycare or school each morn-ing, try to create a peaceful beginning to the day. A child who is ousted from bed and rushed to dress and leave the house will be more likely to resist and beg to stay home than one who is allowed a more relaxed pace to his morning.

To make things easier, prepare as much as possible the night before (set out clothes, pack lunches, set the breakfast table). Plan to get up a bit earlier in the morning to allow an unhurried breakfast together. Leaving sooner for daycare or school allows you to build in a little extra time for dropping off, which means you can get your child set-tled before you need to leave. A calm, peaceful morning sets your child up to be more accepting of the day's routine.

Encourage Your Child to Have Positive Thoughts

Children with anxiety often dwell on their worries. Their thinking becomes negative and inflexible, and they literally talk themselves into feeling more and more anxious. Try to help your child be more open-minded toward possible solutions in all areas of life, and this will carry over into situations of separation anxiety.

To help a child think positively, avoid attacking his negative thoughts or becoming angry with his pessimistic one-track mind. The pressure to *stop* can often cause your child to try harder to convince you of the validity of these thoughts. Instead, introduce new, positive thoughts without judging his previous negative ideas. Encourage your child to look on the bright side and to search for solutions to his dilemmas. Get him started by making positive suggestions and guiding him to be more optimistic in the way he looks at life.

When your child is worried, it's likely that his self-talk focuses on possible disasters: *What if Mommy forgets to pick me up? What if I get hurt and no one is here to help me? What if something bad happens to Daddy while he is away?* A stressed-out child can rehearse these thoughts in his mind over and over until he is overcome with fear and worry. Negative self-talk begins on its own but easily escalates, causing anxiety to increase. It takes practice for a child to change his self-talk to more positive ideas.

The first step is to help him understand that just because he thinks something doesn't make it real. To teach this, wait for a time when your child is relaxed. Use an example to show how thoughts are separate from reality. For example, thinking about a cow doesn't make one appear in the kitchen. Thinking about flying doesn't cause you to take off into the air. Then explain that this also applies to fears, such as thinking that no one will arrive at pickup time or that something bad will happen at preschool.

Professional-Speak

"When an anxious child becomes rigid in her thinking, she is even more likely to be hobbled as she struggles to free herself from her fears."

—John S. Dacey, Ph.D., and Lisa B. Fiore, Ph.D., authors of
*Your Anxious Child: How Parents and Teachers
Can Relieve Anxiety in Children*

You can help your child remember positive thoughts by printing helpful statements on index cards that can be carried in a pocket or backpack. They can be messages such as these:

"Mom always picks me up after school."
"I can do this."
"Everything is okay."
"If I feel nervous, I will take a deep breath, relax, and feel calm."

Play the What-If Game

You can help your child develop more positive ways of thinking by using the What-If game. This is intended to help your child figure out in advance what she will do if things don't go according to plan. By planning this beforehand, your child's stress and anxiety can be greatly reduced.

Say, for example, that your child is afraid you won't be there to pick her up after school. First, let her know that this is highly unlikely,

Madison, two years old

and then (in a reassuring voice) say that even if it did happen, everything would still be okay. Then play the What-If game by defining your child's concerns and outlining the most likely outcomes.

It may help for you to answer the questions first, then ask the questions a second time and let your child answer them. After some practice, your dialogue might sound something like this:

Parent: I know that you worry that I won't be there to pick you up after school. Most likely, I will be there and everything will be fine. But let's play a What-If game. What if you come out of school and I am not there?

Child: Then I could stand and wait five minutes to see if you are late.

Parent: What if you wait five minutes but I am still not there?

Child: Then I could go to the office and ask if I can call you.

Parent: What if no one is in the office?

Child: Then I can go to the health room and ask the nurse to use her phone.

Parent: What if you call me and I don't answer?

Child: Then I can call Dad on his cell phone.

A great children's book series that parallels this kind of thought-tracking process are the "If You Give" books written by Laura Joffe Numeroff and illustrated by Felicia Bond. For example, in *If You Give a Mouse a Cookie*, the little mouse first asks for a cookie, which leads him to ask for a glass of milk. Then he looks in the mirror to see a milk mustache, which leads him to ask for scissors to trim his hair, and so on. You can read one or two of these entertaining books, then introduce the What-If game to your child.

This game is a great way to show your child that it's likely everything will work out okay even if things don't go exactly as planned. It provides her with the idea that there is always another option to find. Finish the game with the reassurance that the What-If things probably won't happen, but if they do, she will be prepared.

Give More Choices

To give your child a sense of control, try to provide a few simple choices leading up to any situation of separation: "Which jacket do you want to wear today?" "Do you want to walk or ride our bikes to school?" "Do you want two kisses and one hug, or two hugs and one kiss?"

Give your child choices about the timing and amount of separation, if possible. Provide choices of babysitters when you can. Give your child options about location, such as whether Grandma comes to your home or he goes to hers. If he can customize his experience, he may be more open to it.

Mother-Speak

"Our morning used to be filled with crying and complaining. Now it's filled with choices like, 'What should we pack in your lunch?' 'What shirt do you want to wear?' and 'Do you want to take your book to school today?' These simple choices keep him moving forward. He almost seems to forget to worry!"

—Sofie, mother of five-year-old Jakob

Using Prayer to Help Your Child Cope

If your child says grace before dinner or bedtime prayers at night, you can introduce a new, special prayer for those times when separation anxiety hits. If you simply instruct him to remember to pray, it may or may not be helpful, because it is unlikely he will be able to come up with the right words under stress. It's better to find or create a prayer that he can memorize or have written on an index card he can keep in his pocket or backpack. You can use any prayer that helps your child, but it should be positive and calming.

There are no rules when it comes to prayer, so it can help if you make up your own verse to address your child's actual concerns. Create a simple rhyming verse that is easy for your child to memorize and recite. Here's one I made up for you; you can revise or edit it to suit your child's needs:

> Please God be with me all day long.
> Make me happy, keep me strong.
> Hold my hand when I am scared
> And let me know that you are there.
> Keep me calm and safe today,
> And chase all of my fears away.

Appreciate That It's Not a Now-or-Never Choice

Your child may not be comfortable attending events, such as play-dates, camp, or birthday parties, and she may choose not to go. In most cases, that's really okay. There will be many opportunities for your child to spend time with friends, go to parties, and participate in other events away from home. Some tentative children will bypass invitations and be perfectly content and comfortable with their decision to stay home. Typically, given enough time, most children will outgrow this phase of separation anxiety and have plenty of experiences away from home.

It is perfectly fine to avoid separating from your child during peak phases of anxiety. It's respectful of your child's feelings and can be easier for all of you. It's fine to take it slow, if you can, so that your child can gradually mature toward independence on her own time-table, with a little nudge of help from you.

Father-Speak

"Our daughter refused to attend parties, visit friends, or play Little League until she was nine years old. Then the dam broke and now she's become a regular social butterfly. I can barely keep up with her schedule!"

—Mark, father of ten-year-old Felicity

Allow Your Child to Bring Something to the Host, Teacher, or Caregiver

If you can encourage your child's relationship with an alternative caregiver, you make it easier for her to stay alone with that person. One way to encourage this connection is to have your child bring a book from home to share or deliver a plate of cookies or a flower to the caregiver. Sharing something with the adult in charge allows an encouraging exchange and creates positive momentum for their time together.

Let Your Child Leave You, Instead of You Leaving Him

Some children prefer to be the ones who walk away in a separation situation. They find it easier to leave than to watch you retreat and walk away from them. It may help to find something interesting and distracting to pull your child's attention off the separation and focus it on the event. Point your child in the direction of something fun, say a quick good-bye, and let him walk away from you.

Talk to the Teacher or Caregiver

Most professionals are experts when it comes to dealing with separation anxiety. Ask for a meeting to discuss your concerns, and come prepared with a list of concerns and possible solutions. Don't talk in front of your child or when the teacher is busy tending to other children or class responsibilities. It's better to ask ahead for an appointment to have a private discussion.

Don't Show Your Annoyance, Frustration, or Worry

It can be frustrating when your child won't go willingly to daycare, school, or a babysitter. It can be worrisome if your child screams because a relative attempts to pick her up or because you've left the

Balin, twenty-one months old

room just to take a shower. However, if you get angry or punish or tease your child, you will likely prolong the anxiety.

When your child is crumbling in tears, it is possible that you are crumbling inside too. You may have concerns about the situation, but it's important that you keep your doubts hidden from your child. Even the youngest child can figure out that you are worried and will assume the situation is bad, dangerous, or just plain wrong.

Be careful about talking about your concerns when your child is within earshot, since you never know what she'll hear. Discussions with your friends, spouse or partner, daycare providers, or teachers should be private.

Preintroduce Your Child to New People

Relatives and friends whom you know but your child doesn't (even grandparents who are seen infrequently) are classified as "strangers" in her book. To prepare your child for times with these people, show her home movies and photos the week before the visit and talk about these lovely people. When they arrive in person, *you* hug and greet them first, so your child sees that you accept and love them.

Mother-Speak

"I put up photographs of our family on my son's bedroom wall. Initially I was trying to reinforce his attachment to his grandparents, who live far away, but I see it also helps him when he is missing his daddy during the day while he's at work. It changes his mood to see happy, smiling faces and starts a discussion about the other photos as well. It is a great distraction that works every time."

—**Amanda, mother of two-year-old Finley**

Reflect Back to Previous Successful Separations

If your child has done well in the past (even after a rocky start), call this to mind: "Remember last time you went to Bible school? You were worried at first, but then you had fun and made new friends. Remember Becky and Kai? I wonder if they will be there today." By reminding your child of situations when she was first worried but ended up feeling good about the situation, you help her call on those memories for a boost of confidence for the current event. Over time her successes in different situations will help her handle new things that come her way.

Let Your Child Take Baby Steps Toward Full Separation

When possible, break down a separation into small, manageable steps. Once your child masters one step, he can move on to the next. As an example, if he becomes panicky when you leave him with a babysitter, start by having the sitter watch your child for an hour while you are home in the same room but busy with another task. Next, have the sitter keep your child occupied while you go off to another room in the house. Progress to a very short stint—perhaps fifteen minutes—away from the house. Advance to slightly longer sessions until you achieve your goal of time away, leaving your child for a full session in the sitter's capable hands.

Relaxation and Coping Techniques: Child-Friendly Ideas

When a child gets anxious or worried, he experiences physical sensations that make him even more uncomfortable. His breathing becomes rapid and shallow, his stomach clenches, his throat tightens, and his body becomes rigid. These physiological symptoms can keep him in an agitated state. You can teach your child ways to relax his body and then to use this approach when he begins to feel stressed. Several different techniques can be used, depending on your child's age and personality.

Progressive Relaxation with the Quiet Bunny

This technique is helpful for young children who have good imaginations. If your child first practices it in a relaxed environment at home, he can then call upon it in times of stress. You may want to start each morning with a brief session that you do together or use it as part of your bedtime routine. Begin by coaching your child through the exercise that I call the Quiet Bunny—here's a sample script:

> Let's be quiet bunnies.
> Close your eyes and relax.
> Breathe in. Breathe out.
> It's time for the bunny to settle down and relax.
> Wiggle your bunny nose. Now make your bunny face be still and quiet.
> Wiggle your toes. Now make your toes relax.
> Wiggle your fingers. Now make your fingers relax.
> (You can add more body parts, such as arms, shoulders, and legs, as needed.)
> Breathe in. Breathe out.
> Relax.
> Now you are a happy, relaxed, quiet bunny.

This can be a helpful technique with children since they can be susceptible to your gentle suggestions to relax. Once your child is familiar with this process, he can repeat it at times when he is feeling anxious.

When separation anxiety hits, crouch down to your child's level, put your hands on his shoulders, look him in the eye, and say, "Let's do our Quiet Bunny." Then talk him through the process. Over time, you won't have to lead him, just mentioning it and asking him to close his eyes will bring about the relaxation.

You can also purchase a tiny toy bunny and allow your child to keep it with him when he is away from you. A key-chain bunny, a bunny bracelet, or a small stuffed rabbit can be used as a visible reminder to rely on the Quiet Bunny method when he feels worried.

Teach Relaxed Breathing with the Bubble Maker

In times of nervousness it is common for a child's breathing to become shallow and irregular; she often breathes through her mouth instead of her nose. This then intensifies the feeling of being out of control and increases anxiety. (Think about that shallow, quick mouth breathing that children often do right before crying.) Teaching your child to recognize this sign and coaching her on a way to regulate her breathing can help her gain control in a situation that is making her nervous.

First, explain to your child that this rapid, shallow breathing is a sign of feeling worried or scared. Tell her that it is something she can learn to control. Demonstrate how this kind of breathing looks, and let her try it so she knows how it feels. Then explain that she can make her breathing slower and more relaxed, and this will help her feel better.

A good way to teach relaxed breathing is to tell her to pretend she is blowing bubbles through a bubble wand—you can even use a real bubble wand to teach her the skills. Your explanation might sound something like this:

> "When you get scared or worried, your breathing might get funny— like you've been running [demonstrate breathing in and out rapidly though your mouth]. This kind of breathing can make you more scared. When you notice that you are breathing like that, you can change it. You can pretend you have a bubble wand, and you are going to blow colorful bubbles. You take a breath in through your nose and gently blow the air out through your mouth to make bubbles float in the air. These bubbles are like magic because they can help you feel more relaxed."

Encourage Independent Play

If your child is happily playing alone, don't feel that you must get involved. It's a good thing for your little one to have some play-alone time. This gives her confidence and demonstrates that she is able to be her own good company. You are not being neglectful if you leave your child to her own devices at times—you are being smart and thoughtful when you allow her some of this independence-building, solo playtime.

Mother-Speak

"Once I started paying attention, I was surprised at how often I imposed myself into Brandy's playtime. I meant well. I wanted to show her I was proud of her for playing on her own but realized that my peeking into her room and complimenting her on her independence were actually reinforcing her need for my presence, just in a different way. Now when I hear her playing alone, I leave her to enjoy the time."

—Barb, mother of five-year-old Brandy

Be Aware of Things That Influence Anxiety

If your child has new stressors to deal with, you may see an increase in separation anxiety, even if it doesn't seem related. Here are some of the things that may cause an increase in overall anxiety:

- Moving or home remodeling
- A sibling starting school
- A new baby in the family
- Parents' divorce or remarriage
- A parent leaving a job or starting a new job
- A friend moving away
- A change of teacher or daycare provider
- Major changes in the daily schedule
- A vacation or houseguests
- An illness, be it the child's, a parent's, or that of a close family member or friend

When children are faced with life changes, they naturally gravitate toward their foundation of safety—you. Since other things may be confusing or different right now, your child may find it reassuring to be at your side. Be patient and a little more responsive to his emotional needs during these times, and he should quickly adjust to his new "normal."

Prepare the House for a Babysitter

If your child will be spending time with a sitter, provide the caregiver with a detailed list of your child's routine, favorite foods, and favorite games. Post a bedtime or naptime routine chart, if either of these will be involved in their time together. The more your sitter knows, the more likely the separation will be relaxed and successful for everyone.

Allow the babysitter to bend some of your regular rules. Having someone new who provides potato chips, candy, or loud dance music, or lets her sleep in a sleeping bag on the floor can give your child incentive to look forward to a repeat visit. The fun of bending the rules can override separation anxiety any day!

Downplay Your Return

If your child struggled while you were away and you return to cover his head with kisses, squeeze him with hugs, and tell him how much you missed him, then he'll get the message that separation is a very big deal. Instead, hold back on the exuberant reunion and stick with a friendly greeting, such as, "Hi, sweetie. Did you have fun while I was gone?" This conveys that separation is a normal situation and nothing to worry about.

If your child wants to tell you about how difficult it was, allow him a brief moment to voice his concerns, but then direct him toward telling you what went *right* instead of rehashing what went wrong. With some helpful questions, you should be able to find out a good thing or two and then focus on those things.

Professional-Speak

"Be open to hearing about how your child feels. However, lengthy discussions about the child's problems are not always helpful and can be experienced as a burden by the child. The focus must be to help your child to be free of worries and fears."

—Leslie E. Packer, Ph.D., child psychologist and author of
Find a Way or Make a Way

Put Gentle, Sensitive Limits on Clinging

There are times when you know your child is capable of being a bit more independent, but habit has him clinging to you far beyond what he really needs. For example, if he continues to follow you into the bathroom long past the time you think it's appropriate, put a gentle limit on what's acceptable. Avoid using negative words like *no* or *don't*, which can just cause him to cling tighter. Instead, use a positive approach to setting limits. For example, you might offer him a choice: "While I'm in the bathroom, you can sit outside the door and do your puzzle, or you can play with your cars in your bedroom. Which would you like to do?"

Mother-Speak

"My daughter didn't want me to leave her until she fell asleep, but I couldn't always stay with her for a half hour. So I developed the phrase 'you go.' I'd let her know when the time was near but let her choose the exact moment, then *she* would tell *me* when to go. She would control the separation. When she was ready and said, 'You go,' I kissed her and left. This still works, although now she says, 'You go,' after a minute and not a half hour."

—Bonnie, mother of nineteen-year-old Ariella, seventeen-year-old Yonina, fifteen-year-old Dovi, thirteen-year-old Mordechai, nine-year-old Yedidya, and four-year-old Liora

Make Sure You Aren't Missing Something

Be certain that your child doesn't have problems with a teacher, caregiver, or another child at school or daycare. It might be a red flag if he shows separation anxiety only in one specific situation but is fine at all other times. Also, be sure your child doesn't have an unrealistic fear or

Zachary, two years old, and Zoe, Madeline, and Mia, all seven years old

belief that is making him anxious. Some gentle questioning and astute observation might lead you to the reason for his concerns.

Be Honest and Straightforward

Sometimes you don't have a choice about separation. Perhaps you've tried your best, but your child hasn't relaxed at all. Regardless of her tears and pleading, you have to leave, and it has to be now. That's the time to be clear, concise, and honest in a respectful yet firm manner: "I must leave now, and I don't have time to linger. Say good-bye now. [kiss, hug] Love you, honey." Later, review the suggestions throughout this book and put together a plan to follow over the next few weeks to help your child deal with separation anxiety issues.

If you've left your child in a safe, loving environment, then depart with confidence. Don't punish yourself with guilt. Focus on the facts of the situation minus the emotion. Move on with your business of the day. Continue to try all the other separation anxiety ideas over the coming weeks, and you'll likely see your child become more confident and independent.

5

Solving Specific
Separation Situations

The ideas in the earlier chapters of this book are tools you can use to help your child work through her separation anxiety. This section will add to your resources to provide you with specific tips for her unique situation. Add what you learn here to what you already know to further customize your plan to help your child deal with those times in life when separation is unavoidable.

Be Observant and Flexible

In any parenting situation there are as many solutions as there are children who need them. Different personalities, diverse family styles, and unique situations all influence your best plan of action. Even after you've devised one, it's key to stay in tune with your child's progress to further refine that plan. Remember, too, that children grow and change day by day, so an idea that might work today could well require an adjustment tomorrow. Parenting keeps you on your toes, but finding that right balance of ideas to help your child leads to some of the most rewarding moments you'll have as a parent.

Make Use of Helpful Children's Books

Reading books to your child is a great way to bring ideas to light, and they can be a perfect way to open conversations. On my website I have provided lists of children's book options that you and your child might enjoy. You'll find a number of suggestions for each specific separation anxiety situation at www.nocrysolution.com.

As a rule, read any book yourself first to be certain it is right for your child. Avoid any that approach the issue from a negative viewpoint or that create new worries for your child by bringing up problems that she hasn't even thought of! Aim for those books that show her that she's not alone in her concerns and that present solutions in an uplifting and encouraging way. Look for those providing specific tips and a happy ending.

Children's stories can be especially helpful since a child can consider her circumstances from a safe distance through a third-person experience as she observes the character in the story. This can make it easier to examine the situation unemotionally and learn some good coping skills.

Lots of Ideas and Many Uses

You might want to take the time to read over all the ideas in this section. Reading about something ahead of time can prepare you for future issues, or you may pick up an idea that will help a friend. Also, an idea listed under one topic can often apply to another; for example, something in the section on babysitters might serve a child who is nervous about attending daycare for the first time, since many of the tips can be modified for use in different situations.

At Home and Out of Sight: When You Can't Leave the Room

A trigger for my son's separation anxiety is when I am in the house but not available to him (like when I take a shower or work in my office). Often he will pound on the door, crying and yelling. I don't answer him because I'm afraid it will upset him more to know that I am there but not coming out. Instead, my husband will tell him that Mommy will be back soon. This doesn't help, and he continues to cry.

This is an amazingly common scenario! Many mothers of toddlers wonder if they will ever be able to use the bathroom again in peace. While it may seem easier not to respond to your child's cries, this can make matters worse, since he thinks that you have disappeared forever. The good news is that children outgrow this phase, and you can move things along by using some of the following ideas.

• **Play the door game.** You can help your child feel better about being on the other side of the door by playing a game. Start by making animal noises. Pick a noisy creature like a cow, lion, or dog. Encourage your child to guess the animal, or just have him echo you. Once he has the gist of the game, then sit him on the floor and go inside the door, leaving it open an inch. Play the game that way and then with the door closed. After that you can play the game when you are in the bathroom and he is outside the door. Not only will he have fun, but it will help him understand that while you are in a room with the door closed you're still there, even though he can't see you.

• **Have practice sessions.** Allow another person to engage your baby in playtime—along with you. Then slowly back up and sit a few feet away. After a little while, get up and leave the room for a few minutes, coming back before your child gets upset and making a happy entrance, "Looks like you two are having fun!" Slowly build up the time to five minutes, fifteen minutes, and so on. A few short practice sessions each day will help your child deal with longer necessary separations.

• **Get your child occupied in play.** Before you leave the room, get your child involved in an activity, then have another adult take over and step back. A great activity for a baby or toddler is looking out the window at the trees or neighborhood, because your child's focus will be outside and away from you. Once the caregiver and your child are engaged, you can make your exit and allow them to continue playing.

• **Allow your baby some independent time.** Look for opportunities to encourage your baby's independent play throughout the day. Often our children are so endearing to us that we don't realize there are times we can and should encourage a bit of independence—it's good for your child to learn that he can entertain himself. Begin to take notice of times when your little one is happily occupied with a toy. When you see this happening, step away from him. If he accepts this, step away a bit farther. If that works, get involved in something, like cooking or working on your computer, so that you can keep an eye on him but be busy with something else. These practice sessions will pay off when you go that one step farther and he can't see you behind a door.

• **Break up your time apart into chunks.** In some cases it can help to break down your separation into parts, coming in and out of the room in segments. Start with short separations and build the time into longer spans as your child becomes used to it. As an example, if you are getting ready for the day, start the process a half hour earlier than needed so that you can pop in and out of view.

• **Create a special box of toys.** Fill a special box with an assortment of appealing toys. Pull it out only when you need to separate, such as times when you are working in your home office or when you are showering. When you are done, close up the box and put it away for next time. Rotate the items in the box so that it always contains something interesting. Make it an exciting part of your routine, and soon your child will be looking forward to it.

• **Bring your child in with you sometimes.** There are times when you need your child on the other side of the door and times when it's less important. As an example, when you are getting ready in the morning, you can have your child stay with someone else when you are showering, then put on a bathrobe and bring your child in with you while you do your hair and makeup. Create a special spot on the floor for your little one to play. Keep in mind that his need to be tied to your side will lessen over time, and you may even miss this once he no longer has to be in the room with you.

• **Allow others to have more time with your child.** Very often a child becomes particularly needy with one parent above all other human beings. This is often because that person tends to his basic needs nearly all the time. If this is the case, that one person (often Mommy) becomes a security object, so it's unfair to be the daily constant in his life and then ask him to separate from you happily only when you need him to.

Daddy Shaun; twins Travis and Jamie, seven weeks old; and Jared, two years old

If you find that nearly all of your child's waking hours are spent with you, try to find ways to have other familiar people spend more time alone with him. Start with short periods and work up to longer spans. Experience will build security, and your child will come to know that others are also capable of meeting his emotional and physical needs—and that they can be fun too.

In order for this idea to work, you shouldn't hover and oversee their time together. Allow them to develop their own rhythm. Provide your child with a supportive comment: "Grandma has you now. Mommy is going to shower." If your child fusses as you leave, don't jump right back in the picture. Allow the other adult to tend to him. It may be different from what you would do, but it's a wonderful gift to allow your child to learn that the world is not filled with Mommy clones. You trust this person, so let her handle this. Get in the shower, go make dinner, or go on your jog, and let the caregiver and your child find their way together.

When your child learns that this person can meet his needs as well as you do, he will apply that concept to other adults as well. And when other people know they can spend time with your child

Father-Speak

"The first time we saw 'mommy separation anxiety' was a few months ago. Jack was having a grand time playing with me. We were laughing and relaxed together. Then Mommy came into the room, and it was like a switch was pulled. He got this unbelievably sad look on his face and started crying. He held his arms out to be picked up by her. We had seen this happen before with my niece, so we were kind of prepared. My niece is older now, and a big-time daddy's girl. So we laughed about Jack's favoritism, realizing that he had entered a new phase and Mommy was now Queen of the Day."

—James, father of ten-month-old Jack

without you hovering in the background, they will relax and enjoy the camaraderie with your little one.

• **Give your child a job to do.** You can assign an older toddler or preschooler a task to do while you step out. Give your child a broom and ask him to sweep the floor, have him sort socks from the laundry, or provide him with paper and crayons and ask him to draw you a picture. If your child feels he is doing something for you and is busy with this activity, it can allow him to part from you for a short time.

• **Use positive self-talk.** Help your child and yourself by keeping your own thoughts realistic. If your baby is in a panic of tears, don't be drawn into the drama and convince yourself that you are doing something horrible to him. You are only going into another room! Your baby is in the good care of another person. It's a great thing for him to learn that the two of you can be apart and the world is still a good place.

• **Understand your child's personality.** Children are unique in how they respond to separation. It helps to consider your child's reactions regarding all things new and different to help determine how to best respond to his needs. Taking cues from his responses in other areas of life can help you figure out the best way to help build his separation confidence.

Babysitter Blues: When Your Child Resists a Babysitter

> **We'd love to be able to go out to dinner or a movie, but the one time we hired a babysitter for our son, we had to sneak out the door, and she said he stood at the window and cried for an hour! We felt like the worst parents ever. Now we're afraid to try again.**

You're not the worst parents ever—actually you're in the running for the best parents ever. Your little one's reaction is a demonstration of the love, security, and comfort he feels when he is with you and that he knows is lacking when you are gone. So first, pat yourselves on the back—you've created a strong and healthy bond with your son.

Since you do have a healthy family, it is perfectly fine—and in fact, good for all of you—for you to leave your child with a babysitter to go out on a date, run errands, visit friends, or even take a jog around the park. The following tips will guide you as you all find peace with this new aspect of family life.

• **Choose babysitters wisely.** Early experiences are most successful when the sitter is someone your child knows well. Try to choose someone who not only loves your child but will be patient with any tears and worries. Your best friend may love your baby to pieces, but if she doesn't have children or any experience caring for them, she may not be successful dealing with the separation anxiety that occurs. An experienced mom or dad (particularly one whose child has suffered separation anxiety) might have more tricks up her or his sleeve to help your little one adjust to the experience.

• **Keep realistic thoughts in mind.** Even though your child is acting like it, you're not sending him to a torture chamber! You're leaving him with a competent babysitter, plenty of toys, and adequate food. Of course it's hard to see him cry and cling to you—but don't let his actions lead *you* to sensationalize the situation. Your calm demeanor will convey to your child that everything is okay, since he trusts your judgment.

- **Start slowly and build up.** If possible, allow your child to ease into the idea of staying with a sitter. You can take steps to build his confidence that everything will be just fine when you exit. For the first session, have your babysitter watch your child while you are still at home. You may even need to start with you remaining in the room—just sit quietly in a corner and try to disappear. Don't comment on any cute things your child does or make suggestions to the sitter. Just be a quiet presence. Once you've done this, have another in-home session but leave the room. If your child follows you, simply return for a few minutes and then try again, popping in and out, and making your exits last a little longer each time. It can help to have a few new toys available for play. Even though it seems odd to pay a babysitter to keep you *and* your baby company, this can be money well spent when your child comes to happily accept the sitter's presence.

After this at-home practice, arrange for a few short sessions where you leave the house for ten or fifteen minutes. When you return, do so quietly. Don't enter the room if your child is crying—he may see this as the way to get you to come back, setting him up to cry longer and harder next time. Instead, quietly enter the house and wait for a happy moment to announce your arrival.

After a few successful practice sessions, you'll be ready to schedule a real event that lasts a few hours. Try to build up the babysitter's time with your child slowly. Even a child who has adapted well might experience a sudden rush of separation anxiety if the period with the sitter goes on too long. This can turn a good thing into a stressful situation or set you back from any success you have had.

Key Point

Once you've chosen a caring, experienced babysitter, take a deep breath and relax. Trust that things will be fine while you're gone. Leave the sitter a phone number, and tell her where you'll be. Ask her to call if she needs you. If she doesn't call—then *enjoy your time away!* You and your child will be back together soon, and this separation is good for your mental health and wonderful for your child's development.

Over time, if you have a cheerful, capable babysitter, your child may even come to look forward to the time with a new grown-up playmate.

• **Leave when your child is well-rested and not overly hungry.** Plan to have the sitter arrive just after your child wakes in the morning or after a nap. A well-rested child will be more flexible than a tired one.

It's fine if your little one is ready for a meal when the sitter arrives—as long as he's not famished. If the schedule works, having them share a meal can be a great icebreaker.

• **Allow time for a relaxed changing of the guard.** Plan ahead so that you aren't rushing around the house, showering, dressing, and giving out instructions the hour before you leave. Progressing from dashing around the house to dashing out the door can intensify your child's anxiety. Perhaps you can invite your child into your room while you are getting ready and bring along an array of toys to keep him happy. Play some peaceful music in the background to enhance the relaxed atmosphere. A peaceful preparation and calm exit mood can filter through to your child's feelings about your departure.

• **Make the actual leaving quick and peaceful.** Set up some interesting toys or a craft activity for the babysitter to use with your child. Once he is engaged with the sitter, say a very quick good-bye and wave with a smile. If things are going well and you interrupt the flow, you'll just call attention to the fact that you're leaving and may set up a fresh anxiety episode.

• **Avoid an in-arms transfer.** Handing your baby over to another adult is a dramatic announcement of transfer and often cues him to object. It can be a more mellow transition if he is playing on the floor or sitting in a swing or high chair when you step away. This way you avoid him being physically "taken away from you." which can cause a jolt of panic. The other advantage to this method is that your child can be engaged in an activity or eating a snack so that he is focused on something other than your leave-taking.

• **Don't come back once you're out the door.** Make sure you have your purse, keys, coat, tickets, and anything else you need. If you say good-bye, leave, and then reenter, you may end up with a double dose of separation anxiety to deal with.

Father-Speak

"We loved the idea of not handing Joshua to his grandmother directly from our arms to hers when we leave, because that's often when he starts to cry. I put him in his bouncy chair, and Nanna started getting his attention by singing and making one of his favorite toys dance. When Alex and I left the house, Joshua barely noticed!"

—**Dean, father of ten-month-old Joshua**

- **Avoid the tear-filled window-waving routine.** How often have you seen a crying child waving good-bye at a window? Some children need this parting gesture and accept the final wave as closure on your leaving. However, in many cases, it creates the agony of watching a loved one drive off. If your child isn't happy with the final window wave, it will be much better to allow him to become involved in an activity and wave you off during the play than to permit a painful last parting.
- **Try a new location.** If you have family or friends with children, see if you can arrange for them to babysit your child at *their* home. Sometimes a new location, particularly one that offers new toys and playmates, can help your child overcome his worries about separating from you. You can also use the step-by-step approach in this situation (as described on pages 30–31), beginning with a visit where you stay but are uninvolved, progressing to a short fifteen-minute session when you're gone, and then adding to the length of separation a bit at a time.
- **Avoid having the sitter take your child away.** Some children feel anxious if they are picked up by the sitter and taken away to another location. In this case, keep your child in his familiar home environment or drop him off at the babysitter's location. It's better than having someone pick him up from home and take him away. There can be something very scary about being removed from your safe haven!
- **Make phone plans with the sitter.** If you want to check on things while you're away, make sure you have a plan. If your answering machine broadcasts your voice in the middle of playtime, your happy

child may suddenly experience a wave of missing you. Or if they are in the middle of a game, story, or falling asleep, you might upset the apple cart by pulling the sitter away to deal with your phone call. It may be better to arrange for the sitter to call you at a predetermined time or for you to send text messages back and forth discreetly.

- **Give your child something of yours to hold.** It may help if you give your child a Magic Bracelet (see Chapter 3) or other token of your love to hold on to while you are gone. Some children respond well if you let them wear your T-shirt or rest on your bed pillow in the evening.

- **Let the sitter bend the rules.** One of the joys of being with a babysitter is getting to do a few things that are out of the ordinary. Staying up late, eating treats, or jumping on the sofa cushions are some of the fun things that can make a babysitter's visit a great experience for your older child.

- **Create a babysitter bonus box.** Put together a box, a drawer, or a cabinet of toys, games, and activities that can *only* be used when the babysitter is in charge. Rotate toys and refresh the selection frequently. Be absolutely firm that these things are used only during babysitter hours, and you'll find this to be a tremendous help in refocusing your child's energy in a fun direction.

- **Avoid leaving a sleeping child.** Almost every parent of a separation-anxious child considers doing just this! However, even if your child normally sleeps all night without waking up, don't give in to the temptation to leave him after he's sleeping. As luck would have it, this will be the one time he wakes up. If your little one awakens to find you gone, it may set you back on any success that you've achieved so far in regard to babysitting.

- **Let your child know what to expect.** A short time before the babysitter arrives, tell your child what's going to happen. Give a

Key Point

Never sneak out on a sleeping child just to avoid the parting tears. You might create bigger problems if he wakes up to find you missing.

brief verbal itinerary and, if you can, include a milestone marker to let him know when you'll be home, such as, "I'll be home after you eat lunch." Don't begin the preparation too soon, though, and don't make it a serious conversation filled with dread, which could build his anxiety. Simply make a cheery announcement a half hour or so before you leave or before the sitter arrives.

- **Don't leave without saying good-bye—even if he's happy.** If you've had some bad experiences in the past and your child is playing happily with the babysitter, you may be tempted to slip out unnoticed. That could net the sitter a few minutes' reprieve, but once your child realizes you are gone, it may create a panic attack. Even worse, once this happens, you may see an increase in your child's separation anxiety because he'll never know for sure when you'll disappear.

- **Be prepared for a replay.** Even if your child had a wonderful experience with a great babysitter, he may not be welcoming when she shows up at your door the next time. This is perfectly normal. Stay calm and allow your child to reconnect with her. Stick around for a few minutes so they can rekindle their bond. Once she has engaged your child's attention, say a quick and happy good-bye.

Don't Go! When Mom or Dad Goes to Work

I'm going back to work in a few months and am worried about how my toddler is going to react when I have to leave him during the week. What can I do to make the change easier for him?

There are many things you can do to prepare your child for your return to work and many ways to handle separation anxiety if it crops up when your work schedule is in full swing. The good news is that the vast majority of children overcome their separation anxiety and adjust to being in daycare or at home with a nanny. It can take patience and a plan, but you can help your child through this major adjustment.

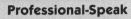

Professional-Speak

"As separation anxiety peaks, you may have real challenges. Don't be surprised if your well-adjusted child morphs into a mommy-obsessed lunatic."

—**Paige Hobey, author of** *The Working Gal's Guide to Babyville*

When you are able to prepare your child in advance for what's to come, you may be able to lessen separation anxiety, although you still may not eliminate it completely. Some of the adjustments will have to happen once the new routine begins. In advance, try a few of these ideas.

• **Have practice sessions.** If your child hasn't had much experience with babysitters, start exposing him to alternate caregivers now. It's good to set something up a few times a week to rehearse for the time when you'll be off to work every day. Even short practice sessions can be helpful. You can use this time for yourself to relax or do things to get ready for your reentry into the workplace: do some shopping, get a haircut, or meet friends for lunch.

• **Let your child practice his social skills.** If your little one will be in a setting with other children, begin taking him to places where lots of children play—such as playgrounds, health club child-care rooms, and church activity rooms. This practice will warm him up to the experience of spending time with a group of other children.

Once you are working, your child may express anxiety no matter how much preparation he's had. That's perfectly normal. After all, what child wouldn't rather have a parent at home than away? The following ideas can help your child work through his feelings and find a new "normal" that is built around your work schedule.

• **Prevent the contagious spread of sad feelings.** Children are amazingly perceptive, and if you feel worried, sad, or guilty about leaving him to go to work, then he'll likely suffer an offshoot of those feelings. Once you've picked a great place or person to care for him, then accept this new life and make the best of it. All types of work and family arrangements function well for children.

Mother-Speak

"I didn't know that leaving my child in someone else's care was going to be so hard for me. When he would cry, it was upsetting and I felt guilty for leaving him. When he would run off to play and barely notice me leaving, I was wracked with jealousy. It's gotten better with time. I suspect that if I had been more accepting of the situation, then Sam would have been also. It seemed that when I settled in, so did he."

—Mother of nineteen-month-old Sam

- **Have very specific routines.** Children feel more secure when their lives have a predictable rhythm. The more they can foresee about their day, the more they can relax in the flow. Set up a specific routine for the following touch points in your child's day:
  — *The morning routine.* How the morning begins can often set the tone for the whole day. Waking at the same time seven days a week and following the same routine for getting dressed, having breakfast, and enjoying early-morning playtime can get your child started with a calm feeling that "today is normal."
  — *The hour before you leave for work.* Whether you leave for work in the morning, later, or at different times each day, the parting routine you create with your child is important. When you have a pattern to your leaving, it allows your child to "switch gears" from one environment (parent home) to the other (caregiver in charge).
  — *The first half hour your child spends with the caregiver.* Once you say good-bye, what happens? Do the two of them play with toys? Have a snack? Read a book? Look at the day's calendar? Engaging in a specific, routine action is much better than your child standing by and watching you walk away. It also helps transition him into this segment of his day. This specific event reconnects your child to the caregiver and sets the pace for their time together.
  — *The reuniting routine.* Create a short but specific coming-together routine. It can be a special handshake, a hug and a tickle, or some other ritual. This takes the pressure off the

reunion, since your child has a certain action he performs. It is also an indicator to change gears—the caregiver is off duty and your time together is beginning.

• **Suggest connectivity projects.** If possible, encourage your caregiver to have your child create something for you during the day. This could be a drawing, a vase of picked flowers, or a batch of cookies. Perhaps have a special box where you place evidence of the day's work that you look through together as part of your reuniting routine. If your child is busy planning and executing the day's surprise or filling his box, it can lift his spirits and help him look forward to welcoming you home.

• **Keep your child busy.** Be certain your child has plenty of toys and activities to keep him busy while you are away. A bored child is more likely to suffer separation pangs than a busy one. If your child stays at home with a nanny, rotate a box of toys for them to use so there is frequently something new for them to discover.

• **Take your child to work occasionally.** Children can feel unsettled if you are gone for long periods and they don't know where you are. It can help to have a short visit to your workplace so your little one sees where you spend your day. Bring a camera, take photos, and make a small album for your child to keep at home. You can even have someone take a picture of you on the phone, frame it, and keep it at home, so your child can see you when you are talking together on the phone.

• **Display family photos.** Have photos of yourself around the house for your child to view when you are gone. If he is in a daycare center, ask if you can display a family photo in his cubby or near where he hangs his coat. In addition, have photos of your caregiver or his teachers in your home so you can show that these people are important to your family.

• **Make your time together count.** Prioritize your life so that the hours you are home with your child are not spent in tasks that keep the two of you separated even longer. For your child to be able to let you go emotionally, he'll need to feel satisfied with the time that you do have. Take a good look at how you spend your time together. Can you include your child in some tasks? Can you find a more time-efficient way to handle some things? Can you cross some unnecessary things off your list altogether?

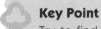

Key Point

Try to find a bit of relaxed time every day to be with your child—playing, taking a walk, reading, or just hanging out together. Those calm moments create a peacefulness that can carry over into busy times.

- **Talk to your child's teacher or babysitter about your concerns.** It is helpful if you talk through any problems and agree to a plan and specific solutions. A qualified care provider will be knowledgeable about separation anxiety and open to customizing a plan for your child. By identifying your specific worries and discussing the options, you can come up with the solutions that are right for your child.

Daycare Distress and Preschool Pains: Making Morning Good-Byes Peaceful

I spent months finding the perfect daycare center for my daughter. It's a wonderful place with kind and loving caregivers, an abundance of toys, a great group of children, and a marvelous play yard. It's been a whole week and my daughter still cries when I drop her off. It is tearing me apart! What can I do?

Heading off to daycare or preschool and leaving Mommy or Daddy behind is a colossal milestone in a child's life. There is no exact method for determining which child will happily wave and run off to play and which one will take one look at the new surroundings and promptly superglue herself to a parent's leg. If yours is one of those superglue kids, here are some ideas to help her loosen her grip and enjoy her new experience.

- **Take small steps to reach your separation goal.** Some children have increased anxiety if they go from a familiar setting to a brand-new situation or a longer separation schedule. It can help to slowly "wean" a child to her new routine. If she is struggling, see if you can arrange to build up to a full day's schedule over time. Begin with a one- or two-hour segment for a few days, progress to a slightly longer period, and eventually to a full day. If you can spread this process over several weeks, it may help your child ease into a full program.

- **Plan for readjustments.** Many children start the week off slowly, but after several days of the school routine, they settle in. Regression can happen after days off, particularly long weekends or vacations. After having three or four days off with you at home, your child has to readjust to the school routine. When getting back into the swing of things after a weekend or vacation, make sure you stick to your normal bedtime, wake up early, and allow the morning routine to be a peaceful one. You don't want to have to hit the ground running after time off. Plan for some quiet time when your child arrives home to unload the stresses of the day. A walk outside, a bike ride, or a trip to the park can do wonders to settle your child into the week.

- **Encourage friendships with home playdates.** Ask your child's caregiver if there are any friends with whom your child has connected. Set up a few playdates with these children at your home. Make each visit relatively short, as too long a visit can be tiring for a child who is new to this kind of socializing. Plan ahead to have a craft or game ready, plus a meal or a snack, as some children will find a full session of unsupervised free time difficult to navigate.

Lindsey, three years old

Once you've had a few successful sessions at your home, branch out to a playdate at a friend's home. At first you may need to stay with your child and visit with the other parent. If that goes well, attempt a short child-only visit while you stay close by in the neighborhood. Let the other parent know that you're fine with a call for an early pickup if things aren't going smoothly. If this happens, let your child know it's okay that she left early. Find something to praise, such as the fact that she remembered to say thank you when she left. Give your child some time and another at-home play session, and then try another short visit at a friend's home.

• **Coordinate arrival with other families.** If you can, coordinate your daily walk or ride to school with another family's. Having a friend along can change the dynamics of the drop-off routine dramatically. If your child resists the idea of the other parent driving, then don't push it—if you're willing, be the sole chauffeur to allow your child this visiting time with a friend. Once they've bonded on the daily drive for a few weeks, then suggest the other parent take a turn and see how things progress.

• **Introduce your child to the school and teacher.** If possible, visit the school building and classroom prior to the beginning of classes. Walk the halls with your child, peek in the classroom doors, and play in the playground. In many cases, it's possible to visit your child's actual classroom and meet the teacher for a casual hello. If time permits, do this a few times before the first day of school. These visits allow your child to view the environment without having the added pressure of being a participant.

This previsit can be a helpful way for your child to begin to picture herself in the classroom. These visits take the mystery out of the new adventure and make the school more familiar when your child arrives on that sometimes-scary first day of school.

Mother-Speak

"Here in Sweden, parents leave the child on day one for one hour, then on day two for two hours, and so on. That way the children come to accept the preschool over time."

—**Patrycja, mother of four-year old Osvald and newborn Asta**

• **Send your child off with a Kissing Hand.** Audrey Penn, in her lovely book *The Kissing Hand*, tells the story of a little raccoon who is afraid to attend his first day of school. His wise mother kisses the palm of his hand and tells him that any time he is worried he can press his hand to his cheek and think, *Mommy loves me.* She explains that her kiss will jump to his face and fill him with toasty warm thoughts.

This is a wonderful idea, because any child can discretely put her hand to her face and receive a boost of confidence anytime she needs it. It also acknowledges your child's fears and lets her know that you understand her feelings and are willing to help her find a solution that will help.

This book takes the next logical step and allows the little raccoon to place his own kiss in his mother's hand so that she too has a special gift to keep her happy all day. This addresses many children's worries about how their parent will fare while they are away.

• **Remain calm when your child is anxious.** When other adults are waving good-bye to their confident children and your little one is crying and clinging to your leg for dear life, it's easy to become flustered. Many parents become sad and worried. These emotions can be zapped right over to your child and increase her anxiety tenfold. It's that time when your child desperately needs you to present her with calm, confident reassurance. Put on blinders and tune out the other parents and children so that you can concentrate only on your child. Focus on the positive aspects of the school and all it has to

---

Mother-Speak

"I really wish that I could stay home and be with Anna rather than work. It is extremely difficult for me to leave her in daycare, and I've found that I need to be careful about communicating that to her. My own separation anxiety has made her anxiety worse. I have to remind myself every day that she is safe and well cared for when she is apart from me. I concentrate on this now during the drop-off time, and I can see that she is doing much better too. What a pair we are!"

—Jen, mother of two-year-old Anna

offer your child. Repeat a positive mantra in your mind: *She's okay. This is a great place. We can do this.* You can be most helpful to your child when you convey a peaceful demeanor to her. (For more tips on parental separation anxiety see Chapter 6.)

• **Be certain you have your child in the right place.** On occasion, separation anxiety issues do not originate from a child's developmental issues but, instead, from a poor fit between the child and the care provider. Those nagging feelings you have may be based on more than just missing your child; they may be intuition that something is not quite right. Perhaps your child isn't quite fitting in or the personality mix between your child and the caregiver isn't jelling. Dr. T. Berry Brazelton, in his book *Touchpoints*, addresses the issue of separation anxiety in a child-care setting:

> It's a good time to evaluate how the caregivers are handling the baby. Drop by at unexpected times. See whether he's happy or not. Look to see whether the childcare providers are sensitive to his rhythms— sleep, play, feeding, and so on. Also, when he looks at them, are they sensitive to him, and do they offer respect and a caring nod? If so, it will help your own separation. If not, it may be time to change.

Big-Kid School Time: Off to Kindergarten or First Grade

My son had a wonderful preschool experience, but he's terrified of starting kindergarten in a few weeks. He keeps telling me he doesn't want to leave me to go to "the big school." I keep telling him there is nothing to be afraid of, but he insists he wants to stay home.

Even if your child has been in daycare or preschool for years, the jump to kindergarten or first grade can be like entering a whole new world. The environment, expectations, and interaction between your child and the teacher and new classmates are all very different from anything he's experienced before. There's also a mystery about the "big school" for many children, who suspect that they will have to do schoolwork that is beyond their ability. In addition, your child's maturity level takes a leap at this age and causes him to examine his surroundings in a more complex way, exposing him to new fears and concerns he didn't have way back when he was "little."

The first step to helping your child overcome his fear is to acknowledge that these are truly valid emotions. He needs you to understand that it's not a simple process for him to put on a backpack and a smile and head off to school. Actually, it may be quite the opposite—just looking at his backpack might start his spiral of doubt, worry, and fear.

You are your child's best ally as he confronts and overcomes his fears. You can help him achieve the confidence to happily join his classmates—but it does take time, patience, and consistent, planned effort.

• **Learn if the problem is separation anxiety or something else.** There are many reasons that children feel anxious about school, and separation anxiety is only one of them. Other possible reasons for your child's apprehension may be a feeling of disconnection with the teacher, concern about the work, confusion about class rules, or difficulty with a classmate. So before you approach your child's fears, it's important to listen carefully to learn his reasons for not wanting to go to school. Understanding his motivation can help you tailor the best solutions for him.

• **Encourage friendship with a classmate.** If you're reading this in advance of the first day of school, try to locate other children in the class. (You might be able to get this information from the school or ask around the neighborhood.) Set up a series of playdates before school starts. Seeing a familiar face on the first day of class can ease many of your child's fears. In addition, being friends allows the two of them to share their concerns and excitement and to realize that they are not alone in their feelings.

If your child has already started school, ask the teacher if there are one or two friends he spends time with at recess or in class. Set up a few playdates at your home first, and work toward having playtime at their homes too. Having a deeper friendship with another child or two in class can create more security during the day.

- **Carpool or walk to school with another family.** If possible, set up your daily walk or ride to school with a classmate or another child who attends the same school but not the same class. If your child resists the idea of other parents driving, then don't push it—you do the driving for a while and try having the other parents take their turn in a few months.

Going to school with a peer can improve the mood of the morning routine, so encourage the bond between them. Resist the urge to participate in the children's conversation other than opening a topic to get them talking. You want to fade away and allow them to talk and connect to each other without your continuous involvement.

- **Meet a classmate at the school.** If you can't arrange for your child to walk or ride to school with a friend, then set up a meeting place at school where they can connect. Try to make this at the front gate, flagpole, or front door so that you can all walk a short distance together, allowing a brief transition from "me and Mommy" or "me and Daddy" to "me and my friend." Walk behind the children, if possible, and let them talk. Steer clear of staying in parent/overseer mode—avoid any admonitions, such as "Slow down" and "Zip your coat," or even reminders, such as "Remember your book order today." You want to fade into the background and be invisible.

If your child won't let go of your hand at first, that's okay. Try to stay quiet and unobtrusive other than to ask a question to get them talking, if necessary. Slowly loosen your grip on your child's hand and try not to interrupt their connection when you leave. Make your good-bye a swift and happy one; aim for a quick hug and a "See you later. Have a great day!"

- **Create a Magic Bracelet routine.** Follow the suggestions in Chapter 3 for using a Magic Bracelet to help ease your child's fears. Using a bracelet for separation anxiety at school has proven to be an amazing aid. Create a send-off routine as you part with your child. It could be as simple as a good-bye phrase and hugging the bracelet— and the arm it is attached to.

If you learn of any other children in the class who are suffering with separation anxiety, share the Magic Bracelet idea with their parents. You might even want to share the idea with the teacher so she can use it to help other worriers in the class. When other children are also wearing bracelets, it can become a tool for bonding among the group and helps your child and the others feel that their emotions are validated and understood.

• **Create a project for together time.** Some children resist going to school because they see it as the end of your days of playtime together. You can demonstrate to your child that it isn't the end— just a change. Set up an ongoing project you can work on each day, such as a craft or puzzle. You can refer to this project when dropping your child off, so she has something to look forward to, or when picking her up. Spending even fifteen minutes on this task after school or a short bit of time in the morning makes it the focus for a bonding opportunity.

• **Approach sick days cautiously.** Children who want to stay home from school because of separation anxiety will often claim to be sick with a headache or stomachache. Parents are put in an awkward position: do you accuse your child of faking illness or allow him to stay home? If you are unsure and choose to let your child stay home, make sure the day really is treated as a "sick day" right up until bedtime. That means limited television and playtime, with the majority of the day spent in bed, listening to music, reading, and resting. A child who is truly sick will benefit from this restful day, and a well child seeking time off from school will become bored and may actually look forward to a return to the classroom.

The New Baby: When the New Sibling's Arrival Affects Big Brother or Sister

> **Ever since we brought our new baby home, our three-year-old has had serious separation anxiety. It's clearly connected to the baby's arrival. Is this normal? What can we do about it?**

Any major change in your child's life can cause him to move closer to you emotionally and physically, and adding a new person to the family is a colossal change! Not only does the family structure alter, but so does your daily routine, the amount of time you have open for

Mother-Speak

"Since the twins were born, Tristan has had more need to be right next to me. I find it completely heartbreaking that I cannot convince him that I would never abandon him. At home it is so frustrating that he must always be with me or be accompanied to another room, especially now that things are always so hectic. I can't go to the washroom myself or put the twins to sleep without him coming to find me, even though I always tell him where I am going and that I will be right back."

—Linda, mother of four-year-old Tristan and ten-month-old twins Talie and Taryn

play, and the emotional atmosphere in your home. It's very natural for your older child to cling to you for support and reassurance. He is likely wondering how this newcomer affects his place in the family and if it will interfere with his accessibility to you. Until all the details are sorted through and your family resettles into its new configuration, it's wise to be sensitive in responding to your older child's separation anxiety.

• **Patience, patience, and a little more patience.** If your child did not suffer from separation anxiety before the baby joined your family, this is apt to be a short-lived phase. If your child had anxiety in the past but has since moved past it, this relapse likely won't last too long, but nonetheless, it can be challenging when you thought you were already past this stage. The best approach is to acknowledge that this is a major turning point for your family and concede the fact that this is going to require some adjustment and settling time.

• **Don't expect him to grow up suddenly.** It's common that when a tiny new baby arrives in the house the firstborn suddenly seems so much bigger and older. Parents sometimes inadvertently change the way they treat their first child—suddenly expecting more of him than they did just the week before. We even refer to the firstborn as "Big Brother" or "Big Sister" even when the child is still a little toddler. At the same time that our perspective changes and our firstborn becomes "big," he is struggling with new feelings that may cause him to feel "little"—regressing in areas of development and needing more of your time and attention. It can help to allow him to grow into those "big" shoes and mature in a slower, normal progression. Try not to push him to be too grown up just yet.

• **Revive old ideas.** If your child had separation anxiety in the past, revisit any solutions that worked for you before. Take a deep breath and call up an extra ounce of patience. Things will never be exactly as they were. Life has changed for your family. In time, everyone will settle in and you'll all find a comfortable new "normal."

• **Aim for short, daily play sessions.** Babies take most of your time and attention, so your older child's sudden separation anxiety may be a plea for more personal attention from you. Giving her even fifteen minutes of uninterrupted attention once or twice a day can help her feel loved enough to let you go when you must tend to the baby's needs. You can even give this time a specific name, such as Mommy-Time, and set a timer for fifteen minutes. Tell your child you can do anything she wants with you until the bell rings. Once she gets the hang of this, she'll look forward to and thrive on these snippets of personal attention.

Sleep: Going to Bed Alone

My daughter seems to have a rush of separation anxiety at bedtime. She cries pitifully if we leave her alone, so we always end up letting her come into our bed. Is this due to separation anxiety? How can we help her be comfortable sleeping alone?

It is possible that this behavior is due to separation anxiety—and it's very possible that it's not. You might *not* be dealing with separation anxiety if any of the following are true:

• She has been joining you in your bed since infancy or for a long time.
• She is always brought into your bed or you lie with her in her bed in response to her fears or tears.

- She relies on you to rock, pat, or otherwise help her to fall asleep.
- She naps in your arms or by your side.
- She always falls asleep in your presence, never or rarely when alone.
- She doesn't display any major separation anxiety issues during the day.
- She is under a year old.

These indicators tell us that your child has a clear preference for sleeping with you rather than sleeping alone. You have become an important component to a good night's sleep. If this is the case, you'll need to create a bedtime plan to change your child's familiar routine. Look for specific ideas on my website at www.nocrysolution.com or in any of my No-Cry Sleep Solution books. In addition, you may find the many ideas for separation anxiety helpful.

Your child's sleep issues are more likely caused by separation anxiety if the following apply:

- She has never routinely slept with you.
- She has always gone to bed easily but suddenly has new fears.
- She starts getting nervous during the bedtime routine.
- She won't go into another room if it is dark or empty.
- She requires your company during the entire prebedtime routine.
- She usually sleeps through the night once she's settled in bed.
- She cries for you immediately upon waking up or rushes to find you as soon as her eyes are open.
- She shows signs of separation anxiety during the day.
- She has passed her first birthday.

The factors in this second list often tell us that a child does not necessarily have sleep issues but, instead, is dealing with nighttime separation anxiety. For a number of children, fear of being alone becomes a cause for these new bedtime problems. Knowing the root of your child's problem can help you fashion the right set of solutions. Regardless of the reason for your child's inability to sleep alone, though, many of the solutions remain the same.

Brielle, two years old; Mommy Jessica; and Aviana, ten months old

- **Understand why separation anxiety affects sleep.** If you think about it, usually the longest separation between you and your child is during her nighttime sleep, when the two of you are apart for eight to twelve hours. Even if you are separated for long hours during the day, other adults and children are with her during that time. She comes to identify sleep as the long separation—the extended period of aloneness.

Professional-Speak

"It is often easier for youngsters to be alone during the day than at night. Refusal to sleep alone is our most common referral. Youngsters who are afraid to sleep alone tend to have difficulty being alone during the nighttime routine [when putting on pajamas, brushing teeth, etc.] as well. As a result, bedtime may become a nightmare for the entire family."

—Andrew R. Eisen, Ph.D., and Charles E. Schaefer, Ph.D.,
authors of *Separation Anxiety in Children and Adolescents:*
An Individualized Approach to Assessment and Treatment

In addition, at night your child will have a number of brief awakenings between sleep cycles, which is a normal aspect of human sleep. When she opens her eyes and realizes she's all alone, this can cause a sudden rush of panic. The same thing happens to her every night, so when she knows that this long separation is about to occur, it may create resistance and struggles at bedtime.

- **Don't make your child "cry it out" to get to sleep.** When she is struggling from separation anxiety at bedtime, these emotions come from a deep need to be with you, because you are her source of security. Handling her nighttime fears by putting her in bed alone and letting her fend for herself, especially when it means tears, does not show your relationship the respect it deserves. Being sensitive to your child's sleep anxiety tells her that she can trust you, and you will be there to help her through difficult situations.

Don't worry about spoiling your child with your love or providing her the attention she needs as she's going to sleep or waking up. The more you meet her attachment needs at bedtime now, the more quickly she will outgrow her anxieties and insecurities.

Professional-Speak

"A child develops trust when his basic needs are taken care of. When a baby goes to sleep knowing that his caregiver will be there for him in every situation, the baby will develop a positive attitude toward the world."

**—Jim Fay, author and founder of
The Love and Logic Institute, Inc.**

- **Minimize separations at bedtime when possible.** It's acceptable for now—better, in fact—to avoid those situations that would have you separate from your child at her bedtime. All too soon, she will move past this phase and on to the next developmental milestone, and a little extra sensitivity will allow her to feel more confident when that time comes.
- **Create and follow a very, very specific bedtime routine.** Your child will feel more relaxed and secure if the evening has a predict-

able pattern. She won't have to guess or worry. I suggest creating a written chart that shows all the steps to bedtime. A poster with drawings, magazine cutouts or actual photographs of your child at each step of the routine is not only useful, but fun and reassuring. Build in plenty of time for a relaxed process that includes songs or music, back rubs, conversation, and reading.

• **Practice with quick, safe separations prior to actual bedtime.** Create situations of brief separation throughout the evening. When you are in the middle of your child's bedtime routine or just after she gets into bed for storytime, take brief trips to another room, such as to get a drink of water or use the bathroom.

• **Provide caregivers with information.** When someone else will be putting your child to bed for naps or at bedtime, make certain this person knows your child's exact bedtime routine. Write it down (or use the poster described earlier) so that the consistency of the night-time ritual can be kept the same as usual.

• **Follow daytime separation anxiety tips.** Helping your child with her daytime anxiety will carry over to easing her bedtime problems. Follow the ideas throughout this book, such as allowing your child whatever separations she initiates during the day. These practice sessions will build her confidence for all separations.

• **Adopt a lovey.** Encourage your child to become attached to a special blanket, stuffed animal, or soft toy that can become a sleeping partner. These lovies can be a comfort to her at naptime and bedtime, since they create a feeling of company and security.

• **Adopt a bedside pet.** A child who doesn't want to be alone at night can often find comfort in a bedside pet, which is a step above a stuffed animal or lovey. The best choices are quiet, low-maintenance pets. A turtle, frog, or fish can make an easy-care roommate for your child. Avoid nocturnal pets like hamsters that run on a squeaky wheel at night! And don't put a dog or cat in bed with a baby or with a child who might have allergies or asthma.

• **Accept one person as the Sleep Queen/King.** Don't take it personally if only one parent is accepted for the bedtime routine. Many children go through a stage of attaching themselves to one parent or the other, and it can be most pronounced when the child is tired. The other parent—as well as grandparents, babysitters, and friends—can find this difficult to accept, but try to reassure them that it's just a temporary and normal phase of development, and with time and gentle patience, it will pass.

If you wish to indoctrinate a second person into the bedtime routine, you can do so in stages. First, have him join you as a quiet observer. Second, have him participate equally. Third, let him take over while you quietly observe. The final step is to turn over the bedtime routine completely. When you do, it's wise if you stay many rooms away and allow your child and her caregiver to find their own comfortable rhythm.

• **Use an imaginary substitute.** If you have an older toddler or a preschooler with a vivid imagination, you can take advantage of this by adding a new step to her bedtime routine. Before you leave the room, give your child a "Little Mommy" or "Little Daddy" to sleep with her. Simply cup your hands as if you are holding something and pretend to give her a tiny version of yourself. Ask her if you can have one of her to take to your own room. If the idea is a hit with our child, this Little Mommy idea can come in handy for daytime separations too.

• **Consider creating a sibling bed.** Children who need human company at night often enjoy sharing a bedroom or a bed with a brother or sister. (One caveat: Don't put a newborn in bed with an older sibling. For safety's sake, wait until the baby is about eighteen months old.) Twins, higher-order multiples, or children who are close in age are often happiest and most at peace when sleeping with a sibling. You may need to stick around and read or tell stories until your children are settled so that this doesn't turn into an evening play session. Many siblings find great joy in sleeping with each other, and it may help to cement early friendships while at the same time solving bedtime separation anxiety.

• **Make use of music or soothing sounds.** Some children find that the dark plus quiet invites scary thoughts. You can fill that quiet space with lullabies or white noise recordings of ocean waves, rainfall, or other soothing sounds to help your child be more at peace.

• **Make a night-waking plan.** Children who suffer nighttime separation anxiety might fight sleep because they don't like waking up alone and scared. If you can set up a plan for middle-of-the-night waking, then your child may be able to relax enough to fall asleep. The plan might involve taking a sip of water, cuddling a stuffed animal, turning on a CD of lullabies, or thinking happy thoughts.

• **Have a presleep chat.** Your child may, for many reasons, be unwilling to part with you to go to sleep. It might help to schedule some time for lights-out conversation just before sleep. Make this part of your tucking-in routine, and allow your child to finish the day by sharing some of her thoughts with you.

• **Include massage in the bedtime routine.** Massage can help promote relaxation, relieve stress, and put your child in a relaxed, sleepy state, making it easier for her to accept your leaving the room. It can also help her fall asleep easier.

Massage is most effective as the last step in the bedtime routine. You'll want your child to brush her teeth, use the toilet (or put on the nighttime diaper), and get that last drink of water before you begin your nighttime rub. Then she can drift off to sleep peacefully after you've helped her to relax.

Regular bedtime massage can help your child associate relaxation and sleep with her bed, and that association is an important factor in helping her fall asleep alone.

- **Finish your child's routine with an audiobook.** While reading is a great way to help a child relax, it does require that you stay in the room. You should definitely continue to read books, since it is such an important component to intellectual development and a lovely bedtime bonding ritual. However, if you want your child to fall asleep alone, then put a limit on the number of books or the length of reading time. When you're done reading, shut off the light and turn on a children's audiobook for independent listening. Listening to a recording in the dark will help your child tune out her worries, relax, and fall asleep.

Growing Up: Attending Playdates and Parties

My kindergartener has been invited to several friends' homes and to birthday parties, but she won't go. I feel like she's really missing out. Should I force her to participate?

At this age, children begin to have formal social events; parties and playdates enter the picture. These are a wonderful way for your child to expand her horizons. However, she has a lifetime of socializing ahead of her and won't be harmed by missing out on a few events until she is ready to take the leap. Many children aren't prepared for a kids-only event until first or even second grade. However, there are things you can do to help a child who really wants to go but needs a little help taking that big step.

- **Rehearsal: Practice, role-playing, and preparation.** Some children suffer separation anxiety because they fear the unknown. They cling to their parents because they are familiar. We can sometimes help children enter an unfamiliar environment by role-playing and teaching them about the situation in advance.

Let's use the example of five-year-old Juan, who has been invited to a number of classmates' birthday parties but always refuses to attend. He receives an invitation to Steffen's upcoming party, and his parents think if he goes, he will see how fun these events can be and overcome his fear. Here's what they do:

Juan's mother first calls Steffen's parents and explains his separation anxiety and lets the other mother know this will be something new for Juan. She asks about the party theme and what the mother has planned for the party.

The next day she tells Juan that they are going to play "the birthday party game" so he can see how a birthday party works. Using their imagination, paper party hats, and newspaper-wrapped toys, they have a pretend party, with Dad playing the role of the party boy. They begin with Juan coming in the door, then they play party games and eat cake, and Dad opens the "presents."

After the game, they talk about Steffen's upcoming party and how it might be the same or different than their game. For the next few

Madison, five years old

days, they casually chat about the upcoming event. Juan's mom has brought home several books from the library about birthday parties, and they read those to further prepare Juan for the big day.

• **Begin with events in your own home.** Children who are nervous about attending an event away from home can work through some of these feelings by first hosting events at home. These pull your child out of her usual routine and introduce new activities into her day. If you've already had several children from her class visit your home, for example, she may find it less unnerving to attend a party where these children will be, since they've already enjoyed social time together outside of the school or daycare environment.

• **Carpool with buddies.** When your child is invited to attend an event, invite one or two of the other children who will be going over to your home for a preparty get-together. Allow them to play together for an hour or so, and then gather them up for a group trip to the event. Since your child has bonded with them, it will be easier to enter the event together rather then stepping into it alone.

Fun Overnight: Attending Sleepover Events

My son is in fourth grade but has never attended a sleepover at a friend's home. He says he's not interested, but I know he's worried about being homesick. I know there's also a second problem. He still sleeps with a tattered stuffed bear, and I know he'd be too embarrassed to take it with him, but he wouldn't be able to sleep without him.

Attending a sleepover is a major milestone in a young child's life. Some kids are ready for this in kindergarten, yet others aren't ready to take the leap until third or fourth grade—or even later. The good news is that sleepovers aren't make-or-break events in a child's life, so whenever yours is ready is the right time for this to happen.

Just because his classmates are ready for sleepovers doesn't automatically mean he is. If it's a truly optional event, allow your child to make his own decision. If it's something more important, such as a Scout camp or a team or school event, then you'll want to encourage

Professional-Speak

"Your child *does* need to confront separation-related situations. But it's important to understand that children have to confront their fears at their own pace. If you push too hard, your child may shut down and refuse to make any effort at all."

—**Andrew R. Eisen, Ph.D., and Linda B. Engler, Ph.D.,**
authors of *Helping Your Child Overcome*
Separation Anxiety or School Refusal

your child to attend if possible. As you encourage him, be sensitive to the fact that this is beyond his comfort level and work to find ways to make it easier for him.

If your child would love to attend a sleepover, but fear, worry, or separation anxiety is standing in the way, use the following tips to help him along.

• **Consider a schedule revision.** If there are options, consider a twist on the planned schedule. Perhaps your child can attend the event but leave early before bedtime. This will allow him to be in on the fun and enjoy part of the experience without worrying about bedtime.

• **Have a rehearsal.** To help reduce the stress of the unknown, you might have a mock sleepover at your own home. This dress rehearsal can help you talk your child through all the aspects of the event—from getting ready for bed in a strange home, to how to phone you if he's worried or nervous. Teach some "good guest" manners, such as putting his dishes in the sink, making his bed, and being polite. If you can change your child's focus to the mechanical details of the event, you can eliminate some of the uncertainty.

• **Have your child be the host first.** Before sending him off to sleep at someone else's home, have him host a sleepover at your home first. This event allows him to veer from the usual bedtime routine and see what it feels like to have a sleepover with a friend, all in the safety of his own home.

• **Choose the host family wisely.** It helps to search out a playmate whose parents have a similar parenting style to yours. If your child becomes fearful at bedtime or wakes up in the night, you'll want the host to be a compassionate parent who will reassure him and gently help him back to sleep.

A good first sleepover is often one at a grandparent's or other relative's home. This is especially helpful if your child is very familiar with their home. A successful overnight experience with a family member can build a child's confidence to try a sleepover at a friend's home.

• **Choose the place wisely.** For early experiences, try to find a home that is similar in atmosphere to your own. If you have a houseful of kids who share bedrooms, dogs roaming the halls, and a television playing in the evening, your child may be out of place in a very quiet home with one child, no pets, and silence after the bedtime ritual. Conversely, if your home is quiet and reserved, your child may be overwhelmed in a house full of noise and people.

• **Send your child's lovey along with him—in a secret place.** An older child is sometimes embarrassed to take along his blankie or teddy bear to sleep with, but unable to sleep without it—especially in a new environment. The best solution is to have him take his own pillow or sleeping bag and tuck his lovely inside. That way he won't be broadcasting its presence but will still have it along to reassure him and help him sleep.

• **Give him a way to share the event with you.** Express your interest in the event and tell your child you'd like to know more about what he does. Send him along with a notepad and pen so he can jot down what he's doing, or send a disposable camera with him so he can take a few photos. Having this mission might help him see the event through your eyes, making it much more fun for him.

• **Manage bedwetting for a sleepover.** If your child wets the bed, you'll want to have all the details of a plan in place beforehand. Purchase special pull-up disposable pants that look like real underwear. Set a plan for your child to change into his pajamas in the bathroom and use pajamas that are baggy rather than slim-fitting pants (or a nightgown for a girl). Suggest that he reduce liquids after dinner, avoid soda pop, and use the bathroom twice before going to sleep. Pack a second pair of pants for a middle-of-the-night change and a gallon-sized baggie to carry home any wet pants so they don't have to be left in the trash.

• **Suggest a unique sleeping place.** If, at the sleepover, the children sleep in regular beds in a bedroom, it may be a little too much like home but different enough to cause homesickness. A better location for a sleepover is often in sleeping bags in the family room or on the floor in a makeshift tent. The uniqueness of the location can help overcome sleeptime worries.

• **Have a call-home plan.** Most children feel better if told they can call you to come home by a certain time of night. They can tell the host's mother, "I don't feel good. I'd like to call home," which is true since "not feeling good" covers emotional suffering as well as physical pain. You can even have a code phrase for your child to say if he's changed his mind and wants to come home. Talk over the event the next day and let your child know that he did well by trying and staying as long as he did. By avoiding negative feedback about aborting the sleepover plan, you encourage him to try again.

Bon Voyage! Planning a Successful Adults-Only Vacation

We have an opportunity to stay at a friend's home in Hawaii—just the two of us. Grandma and Grandpa have offered to watch our children for the week. I have mixed feelings. I'm excited about the trip but find myself sick with worry about the kids' separation anxiety—so much so that I'm actually considering canceling our trip!

Once you become a parent, every decision is colored by your relationship with your children. You are certainly not the first person to consider passing on a wonderful opportunity to avoid causing your little ones emotional stress. However, if you have set up loving, responsible, willing, and familiar caregivers for your children, don't let uneasiness prevent you from taking advantage of this chance. It may take a day or two and several phone check-ins for you to relax, but this may likely turn out to be a wonderful time for everyone involved.

Mother-Speak

"When I told my daughter I was going out of town for a few days and Nana and Papa were coming to visit, she was very upset. I reminded her that they had stayed with her many times and told her stories about what they had done. By the time Nana and Papa arrived bearing cookies, she had forgotten about her sadness! After I said my good-byes, I had her start a game of hide-and-seek with Nana and her little brother, so they were all occupied while I slipped easily out the front door."

—Sarah, mother of three-year-old Alasia and
one-year-old Mattias

• **Find a creative way to say good night.** Lots of children's books use the moon or stars, common objects that everyone sees at night, as a way to pass good nights over the miles. The potential problem with this is that your children may go to bed before dark or may not be able to see the moon or stars on cloudy nights. It's best to find a foolproof method of delivery for your special good-night message. Here are a few ideas:

— Frame a family photo to place at your children's bedsides.

— Record a good-night song or message to be heard at bedtime.

— Give your children a card with a "sweet dreams" message written on it.

— Put one of your shirts on a stuffed animal for bedtime cuddles.

Have the person in charge handle this good-night ritual very early in the bedtime routine and not right before lights out, when it might bring a rush of separation anxiety that you don't want occurring right before sleep.

• **Determine the emotional value of phone calls.** Some children love to receive phone calls from parents who are away. Others find it causes them to miss their parents even more. If your children enjoy calls, make them brief and cheerful. Tell your children something interesting. Avoid general questions like "How are you doing?" and instead ask specific questions about something they have done, such as "Grandma told me you baked cookies. What kind did you make?"

Josephine, three and a half years old, and friend

• **Make a photo book.** Before the event, put together a photo album with pictures of the family doing fun things together. Your children can keep this album as their own to look at whenever they like.

• **Make a storybook recording.** Tape record yourself reading books to your children. For younger children, you can read from picture books. Use a small bell or other sound to signal page turning. That way your little ones can look at the pictures as your voice does the reading.

You can plan ahead and record your daily reading time—this can then be left with your children to listen to whenever they like. Children do like to hear stories more than once, and as a bonus, when they hear their own voices on the tape along with yours, it will conjure up memories of when you made the recording together.

Bedtime is a logical choice for playing the tape, but it is not always the best time, because hearing your voice could create stronger feelings of missing you. Then again, some children are comforted by a parent's voice at bedtime. Have your caregiver gauge the best time for this recorded storytime for your children.

- **Set up playdates and activities in advance.** Prior to leaving, arrange to have a friend come for a visit, or if your children have done it before, arrange for them to go to a friend's house for a playdate. Check into any local events that might add some fun to the time you are gone. If the caregiver can take your children to the zoo, a puppet show, bowling, or some other event, it can add a distracting bit of fun and a refocus of emotion toward positive things.

- **Instigate a creative activity.** Leave supplies for the caregiver to help your children create something for you while you are away. A "welcome home" poster or a booklet of pictures about the time you've been away are great ideas that can take many days to create and will get your children excited about making something special for your return. They might also bake cookies or some other treat on the day before you arrive home. Doing something for others gets children thinking toward the joy that they will be providing you when you return.

Military Duty: When a Parent Is Deployed

My husband has been called to join his unit. How can we get our children ready for this, and how do I help them deal with missing their daddy while he is away?

Deployment is a challenging time for parents and children. Little ones don't really understand what's happening—but they do know that Daddy or Mommy is leaving. Young children have little real concept of time, so they don't comprehend when their missing parent will return, and it may seem like a long, long time until then.

It's helpful to take advantage of the support you can get from other military spouses, so you can share ideas. In addition, if you can connect your children with other military kids, either in person or as pen pals, then your children will feel their situation is normal. They'll also gain support from these friends. Check with the office of your spouse's branch of the military and ask if there are family programs that can provide support and ideas for you.

Here are things you can do to get your children ready for a parent's leaving.

• **Give them a simplified version of the facts.** They don't need all the details, but they do need to know that their parent is leaving to do an important job, to help other people, that he will be back, and that they will be taken care of by other capable people while he is away.

• **Acknowledge your children's emotions.** Children may have conflicting feelings. Let them know that it's okay to be sad, scared, or angry about this. But also let them know that they can work through the feelings and still be happy and have fun—even when they are missing Daddy or Mommy. Don't assume these feelings are there, though. Ask questions rather than acting on what you suspect may be the case, so you have a clear understanding of your children's feelings and can address them accurately.

• **Create a visual time line.** If you know when the traveling parent will return, create a countdown calendar. This can be an actual calendar, a bulletin board with a token to represent each day, or a chain of paper clips hanging on the wall. Make it a daily or weekly routine to update your time line.

• **Put together a Daddy/Mommy Box.** Get a big box and glue the absent parent's picture on the front. Have Daddy or Mommy fill it with small tokens before leaving, such as plastic animals, stickers, or lollipops—one prize for each day or week that he or she will be gone. (Check a birthday party supply store for a variety of inexpensive token prizes.) Make it a fun ritual for your children to gain a small prize from the box, perhaps when you update your calendar. If the return date isn't specific, you can still have the box, just refill it as needed.

• **Keep daily rituals and routines the same.** Continue your typical morning and bedtime routines. Serve the same foods as usual and play the same games. Avoid introducing anything new during this time, if possible. Keeping these familiar touchstones in the day will prevent your children from having to deal with too many changes all at once.

• **Create a storybook recording.** Before a parent leaves, have him tape-record himself reading books to your child. For younger kids, read from picture books and label them to match the recording, ring-

Daddy Adama and Jasmyne, five years old

ing a bell when you turn pages—that way your children can look at
the pictures as they do during an "in-person" reading. For older children, read from an age-appropriate novel, or plan ahead and record
your daily reading time. You can even alternate reading a page each,
parent and children, so that as a bonus, when they hear their own
voices on the tape and the laughter or comments between them, it
will conjure up memories of when they made the recording together.

• **Let other caregivers know the news.** It's important that daycare providers, teachers, and close friends all know what's up so they
can be on the lookout for behavioral changes and provide emotional
support to your children.

The following ideas can be helpful in dealing with separation
anxiety while a parent is away.

• **Expect more clinginess or neediness.** Children missing one
parent may expect more emotional support from the parent still at
home. Try to be patient when your children need a double dose of
your time and attention. Over time, your daily routines will enable
your children to adjust, and the clinginess should dissipate.

• **Create a tangible representation of connection.** Since parent
and children won't be together physically, you can create something

that represents a connection between them. Stephanie Skolomoski, in her children's book *A Paper Hug*, suggests tracing a child's handprints, cutting them out, and connecting them with a string so that the missing parent can have a hug from the child anytime he wants one. I'd suggest that the parent who is leaving do the same thing—create a hug to leave with your children. If you're crafty, you might even choose to make the hug more nurturing by making the hands out of fabric or crocheting two hand-sized pads with a chain between. If you keep the chain extremely short, this can even be used as a bedtime buddy.

• **Help your children keep a diary.** A "diary" can be as simple as a shoebox filled with drawings and mementos of things they are doing while their parent is away. This allows them to look forward to the parent's return so they can share all the tidbits that have been collected. Upon his return, this will provide them with a tangible way to reconnect as the children explain all of the things inside the box.

• **Convey feelings of confidence and peace.** Even the youngest baby can pick up on a parent's emotions. Try to keep your own feelings in check around your little ones so they don't become worried. Take care of yourself and find time to spend with family and friends so that you can be wholly present for your children.

Family Changes: When Parents Separate, Divorce, or Remarry

Our divorce is bringing up many problems for our children. They are very close to both of us. The move between two separate homes is bringing out separation anxiety no matter which home the kids are at. How can we make this easier on them?

Everyone knows that marriage issues affect children, and many things must be ironed out before the new family arrangement falls into place. It can take a long time for your children to get used to things, like going back and forth between homes and parents, and it takes time for you to settle into the new routines yourself. The following tips can help you as you assist your children in dealing with their separation anxiety throughout this adjustment period.

• **Acknowledge your children's feelings.** Most likely, your children miss the absent parent and are confused about the new state of the family. Your understanding of their pain can help them make a more complete adjustment. If possible, find a support group of children of similar families so they can share experiences. Children won't always talk specifically about their situations, but their similar lifestyles will create a feeling of normalcy for them.

• **Have two Magic Bracelets.** The Magic Bracelet idea outlined in Chapter 3 can be a significant idea for helping your children connect with their absent parent. This can reassure your children that both parents love them, no matter where they are. I suggest two completely different bracelets—one representing each parent. It will be important to have a backup duplicate for each bracelet at each home, since your children could find this to be a key to their peace and an important way for them to feel both parents' presence no matter where they are. You might even find it helpful to have your children wear both bracelets at all times to give them a feeling of unity with both parents.

• **Create doubles.** The more you are able to duplicate your children's important things, the easier it will be for them to adjust, since they won't forever be missing something that's at the other home. Even if you plan to carry things back and forth, your schedule may not always permit retrieving them, and of course, items will be for-

> **Professional-Speak**
>
> "Divorce is not a single event, but rather a process that unfolds over months, years, or even decades. This unfolding process will be like a journey along a trail with many unexpected bends and forks. Many people inaccurately estimate how easily and quickly they will adjust to their divorce."
> —**Nicholas Long, Ph.D., and Rex Forehand, Ph.D.,**
> **authors of *Making Divorce Easier on Your Child:***
> ***50 Effective Ways to Help Children Adjust***

gotten and misplaced when shifting between homes. Here are some examples of key items that are worth duplicating:
— Lovies or favorite stuffed animals, toys, or dolls
— Pillows, blankets, or bedding
— Potty chairs, high chairs, and swings
— Favorite baby bottles or pacifiers

• **Have similar pets at both homes.** It can be reassuring for your children to have the same type of pet at both homes. Having a live pet—like a cat, fish, hamsters, or turtles—in both bedrooms can tie the places together and be a familiar component in building a duplicate daily routine in both places.

• **Set up a plan for cross-communication.** It is helpful to have specific ways for your children to reach the other parent to talk when needed. Teaching them how to make their own phone calls and send text messages and e-mails, as well as giving them access to methods to reach their other parent can give them the security to know they can contact either of you whenever they like. If the other parent lives in a different state or country, also provide your children with writing paper, prestamped envelopes, and small boxes for mailing mementos or surprises.

• **Create a specific daily routine.** Children function best when their days are predictable and consistent. Your little ones will feel less anxiety if their daily routine is the same no matter which home they are in. That means having a consistent time for waking up, meals, playtime, and sleep. It also means following the same bedtime and mealtime routines and having similar expectations for behavior in both places. The more you can write down about these routines and post them in both homes, the easier it will be to stay consistent.

• **Deal with your own separation anxiety.** You will be missing your children when you are apart. It can help to keep an open dialogue with a trusted friend, family member, or a counselor so that you can sort through your feelings and find the best way to deal with them. This won't be a one-day conversation; it will be an ongoing process over a period of many months.

• **Keep your children out of the middle.** It can be especially difficult for children to hear negative things being said about a parent they desperately miss. Not only can this cause an increase in separation anxiety, it adds a layer of guilt for them, making them feel disloyal for loving and missing that parent. Do your best to keep your negative comments away from your children.

• **Search out the support you need.** This book can only touch on this significant topic; you'll need more than a few pages of ideas to help you and your children adjust and settle into a new "normal." It can be very beneficial to connect with other parents whose children are in a similar position. Online and in-person support groups can be extremely helpful as you navigate your way through this new chapter in your lives.

Gone Again: When a Parent Travels for Business

> My husband just accepted a promotion that means he'll be traveling regularly for work. How can we help our children deal with this change in our lifestyle?

When a parent travels frequently, children can easily adapt and accept this as the "normal" way that your family works. The key to making this work is to plan how you'll be handling the separations and then stay consistent with the ways you keep your children and the absent parent close in heart when they are apart in person.

• **Construct travel-time rituals.** To make travel time a routine part of life, try to develop rituals surrounding the leaving, the time away, and the return. Create an age-appropriate way for your children to monitor the number of days the traveling parent will be gone by using a sticker chart, a paper chain, or a calendar. Once they are accustomed to this method of tracking days, it will be a helpful visual to gauge comings and goings.

• **Have a regular communication plan.** Develop ways to keep parent and children connected over distance using text messages, phone calls, or e-mails. To make phone calls more productive with young children (who often find them awkward), use a speakerphone so that both parents can be involved in keeping the conversation going. This is also helpful if a little one loses interest or wanders off because he can hear both parents conversing and just finds comfort in the sound of the traveling parent's voice.

• **Be positive, not apologetic.** All parents have different work schedules, and children adapt to the differences. Work travel should be presented as a normal, interesting part of your job. Don't dwell on the aspect of separation or leaving. Tell interesting stories about where you've been and what you've done.

• **Let your child pack a toy in your suitcase.** As part of your packing ritual, let your children choose a small toy to send along in your suitcase. Knowing that a small piece of them is traveling with you can be fun and bring them a sense of connection with you.

• **Begin a collection.** Bring home small tokens from wherever you've been. These shouldn't be elaborate gifts, just small mementoes of some sort, such as a magnet, keychain, or postcard. This gives your children something special to look forward to whenever you return home.

• **Make playtime a priority when you are home.** Your children don't need you to be a constant companion when you are home, but do schedule regular and consistent playtime. Young children can benefit from even an hour per day of undisturbed time with a parent who travels frequently. This one-on-one connection can have lasting effects to keep you all close.

Father-Speak

"I travel around the country for work. We have a large wall map, and my wife puts a small photo of me on the map and a countdown of days until I'm home. The kids cross out each day, and it helps them look forward to my return. I always bring a postcard of the place I have been, and we add it to the collection taped up on the wall near the map. They always look forward to it."

—**Ryan, father of seven-year-old Hannah and four-year-old Evan**

Natalie, twenty-two months old, and dog Barney

Playmate Parting: When Older Siblings Go Off to School

Our oldest is going off to kindergarten in the fall, and I'm worried about his younger brother. The two of them play together constantly, so I'm sure the little one is going to really miss having his brother at home. Any tips for handling this transition?

Many young children have wonderful relationships with a slightly older sibling who is suddenly off to school every day. When a beloved sibling is suddenly gone for hours, it can leave the little one with a unique kind of separation anxiety, different from when a parent is gone. Many adults fail to spot the younger child's reaction as they are so involved in getting the older child ready and off to the new school adventure. Then, just when they feel they'll have more quality time with the little one, they confront an array of baffling behaviors—such as temper tantrums, whining, or sullenness—that they are unaware are related to the change in the relationship between siblings. It just takes time and a few tips for your child to adapt to this new daily routine.

- **Value and protect sibling playtime.** If possible, allow the two of them to reconnect immediately after school. Try not to schedule homework, dinner, or other tasks too soon after his sibling arrives home. Let them have a bit of unstructured playtime together so that your little one can meet his needs to be with his sibling.
- **Keep your little one busy.** A busy child is less focused on missing his sibling, so keep him active. Toys, games, or helping you with household tasks will keep him on the go, particularly during transition time, such as the hour after his sibling leaves the house.
- **Visit the school.** Young children can be unsettled by the fact that an older sibling leaves the house for long periods of time and goes to an unknown place. To help your child visualize where his older sibling goes all day, make a few visits to the school. Let your little one walk the halls and play on the playground. Whenever you drive by the school, make a comment, such as "There's your brother's school!"
- **Let him know he'll get a turn too.** Your little one may feel left behind during all the excitement of setting up your older child for school. Talk about how school will be a place for him too, when he gets bigger. Allowing him to be part of the planning can help him feel like an active participant in the process. Let him help pack a lunch for his sibling or color a picture to put in his sibling's backpack. This can also help him know that his older sibling won't forget about him when they are apart.
- **Set aside special one-on-one time.** Your little one might adjust to these life changes more quickly if he sees that this new routine allows him more special time with you. Whether the two of you are playing at home or running errands together, take advantage of the bonding opportunity. For a younger sibling who has not had much solitary time with a parent, this new aspect of his day can hold some very special meaning for him.

6

Parents' Separation Anxiety

New parents are often taken by surprise by the intensity and depth of their connection to their child. They expect love, of course, but the passion that fuels that love is much more than most people ever expect. It exposes them to emotions they never knew they could have.

These love emotions are the fuel that brings out your instincts to protect your child. When your little one is outside your control, these are the emotions that create your own separation anxiety. These feelings of loss of love, loss of control, and loss of companionship well up inside you when you hand your baby over to a sitter or when you watch your preschooler hop aboard a school bus and ride away. Your emotions can run the gamut from uneasiness all the way to outright panic.

The best way to handle your separation anxiety is first to acknowledge that it is a normal aspect of parental love, with roots in the strong natural connection between you and your child. Second, take the steps to be sure your child is in good care when you are apart. Finally, allow yourself times away from your child without worries or guilt.

The best way for me to provide you with information on this sensitive and complex topic is to let my test parents do the talking. Their experiences and feelings are genuine, and I believe you can learn some very important things directly from them. The parents' names have been withheld in this section to allow them to convey their feelings totally and honestly for this book. I hope that their stories will be helpful and reassuring to you.

> "Your own feelings can be so extreme that it can be shocking and catch you off guard. I never thought it would affect me like it did. The first time I went on a trip without my daughter, I cried off and

on for two days. I couldn't even talk on the phone to her or to my mom, who was taking care of her. It was just too hard and painful."

> —*Mother to three-year-old Caitlyn and*
> *one-year-old Donovan*

"The first time I left Lilly for a few hours, she was an infant, and I felt paralyzed with worry. I only went to get my hair cut, and the entire time I was there all I could think about was her. I was anxious to go home and even told the stylist I was late and couldn't take the time for her to finish styling my hair! I needed to rush home because I was starting to panic."

> —*Mother to nine-month-old Lilly*

"The one day that really shows how much separation anxiety I had was the first day I went back to work. I woke up that morning feeling anxious, because I knew today was the day and there was nothing I could do about it. I got Hazel ready to go to her grandmother's house; I couldn't stop hugging and kissing her all morning. When it came to the big moment of putting her in her grandmother's car . . . wow, what a rush of butterflies to the stomach. I strapped her in, kissed her good-bye, and closed the door.

"Walking back into the house was the strangest feeling, because it was probably the first time in a year that I'd walked into a silent, empty house. The whole time I was getting ready for work I felt like I was just walking in circles, not knowing what to do! The anxious feeling and butterflies didn't go away until I was actually working; then I was too busy focusing on what was at hand to think too long about my daughter. Whenever I had a break, though, I was thinking of her.

"When I got home, I learned that she did fine all day. Not even any crying. I had a rush of relief, yet, amazingly, that relief was tempered with sadness that she really didn't need me there all the time."

> —*Mother to fifteen-month-old Hazel*

"I feel that my own feelings of emptiness and worry when I am apart from my children are very normal for any loving mother. The relationship with one's children is one of protector, provider, and nurturer. I have made peace with those emotions."

> —*Mother to two-year-old Madeline and seven-*
> *month-old Benji*

Jared, two years old

"I never would have expected it, but when my little buddies are gone, the house feels weirdly empty and much too quiet. I can't wait for them to get back."

—*Father to five-year-old Owen and three-year-old Stephen*

"I now find myself a single mother of two children with virtually no free time to myself. However, just recently my parents came to town to take care of the kids while I went away for the weekend, and the minute I was out the door I felt free. That feeling lasted about one night, and by the second night I was so sad. I was missing both my children so very much. I enjoyed myself and was so thankful for the opportunity to sleep without being woken by one or the other child, but I can honestly say I didn't feel at peace until I was back at home with them."

—*Mother to four-year-old Alasia and two-year-old Mattias*

"Our son has usually slept in our bedroom on a futon. We all read together before bed, and when we turned out the light, he just stayed there. Recently he stopped this routine and has been going into his own room every night. I always felt he should be sleeping in his own room, but now that he's actually doing it, I'm stunned at how much I miss having him with us."

—Father to eight-year-old Jacob

"I had to answer 'never' to all of the questions on the separation anxiety survey because I have never been away from my daughter on a business trip or a vacation or even an overnight. Maybe *that* says something about my separation anxiety."

—Mother to four-year-old Maria

"My anxiety comes from the awareness that his safety is at risk when he is with someone else, even his daddy, who can be more relaxed than I am. Lucas is very quick and curious, and as you know, it takes only one second to lose track of a toddler! I fear sometimes that Daddy might get to talking or working on his computer and not realize Lucas has discovered something interesting but dangerous. I am always relieved when the day is done and we are all home and safe together."

—Mother to two-year-old Lucas

"My anxiety is the main problem—hers is secondary. I know that it is normal for her to feel separation anxiety, but the feelings that she picks up on from me worsen her experience. It is so hard for me to leave her. It seems that leaving her somehow means that I'm abandoning her, even though in my brain I know I'm not."

—Mother to three-year-old Lis Ana

"Being a stay-at-home mom, I'm around my daughter almost 24/7. I feel like I'm the person who knows her best—I understand the few words that she says, and I know what she needs. It's hard for me to hand her over to anybody else. In my mind, I know everything will turn out fine, and my daughter enjoys staying with others, but in my heart, it's so hard to let go. To be honest, I really take pleasure in being needed by my child, because I've never been needed like this before in my life. It doesn't feel like it's a sacrifice. I know it won't last forever; she's only young once."

—*Mother to eighteen-month-old Elisa*

"When I took my firstborn child to nursery school (when he was two), I used to get stomachaches every morning. His caregiver was trying to comfort me, saying what a great time he was having there and that he actually stopped crying the minute I left school. She knew, though, that I was still very worried, so she gave me a CD with pictures of my son at nursery school (taken throughout the day) showing him having a great time. I browsed through the photos with tears in my eyes and had the pictures set as the screensaver on my computer at work so I can look at his smiling face every day!"

—*Mother to four-year-old Nicolas*

"I recently sent my five-year-old daughter to her first 'slumber party.' She stayed the night with my cousin who has a daughter her age. I did not want her to go at all! I felt so blue the entire evening. Even though I knew she was having fun and in good care, I didn't sleep that night because I was feeling her absence from the house."

—*Mother to five-year-old Isabella*

"This is what I consider *for me* to be 'healthy' maternal separation anxiety: having a great time being away but missing her like crazy, talking about her to others, looking forward to seeing her as soon as I get back, and a feeling of euphoria when we are reunited."

—*Mother to twenty-two-month-old Annika*

The Test Parent Survey

The separation anxiety test parents completed a questionnaire about their own emotions when separating from their children. Knowing that others feel the same way as you do can be very reassuring. The following chart provides a summary of their shared experiences:

Test Parents' Adult Separation Anxiety Questionnaire Summaries

Reaction to Separation	Never	Once	Occasionally	Many Times
Felt sadness in my heart when I left my child	0%	0%	39%	61%
Worried about my child even when he/she was left in good care	0%	3%	42%	55%
Rushed through something to get back to my child	10%	9%	40%	41%
Made an excuse so I didn't have to leave my child	16%	9%	35%	40%
Turned down an invitation because I'd rather be with my child	15%	6%	47%	32%
Felt physical pain (e.g., stomachache) from missing my child	52%	8%	24%	16%
Felt guilty for leaving my child when he/she was crying	5%	16%	29%	50%
Felt like I was doing something wrong when I left my child	26%	8%	29%	37%
Was surprised by the strength of my own separation anxiety	9%	3%	45%	43%
Felt that I am the only one who really understands my child	8%	8%	41%	43%
Cried when we separated due to my own feelings about parting	34%	37%	13%	16%
Felt great relief when we were reunited	8%	3%	26%	63%

The No-Cry Separation Anxiety Solution © Better Beginnings, Inc.

Tips for Parents Who Feel Separation Anxiety

I suspect that you see yourself in some—if not many—of these parents' comments. The test parents in this group are from all over the world, and they have children of varying ages. Their families are of every imaginable makeup. From this I have learned that no matter the differences, we are remarkably alike in many ways. As you can see, a parent's separation anxiety is very normal, and it can be a big challenge. No matter if your anxiety is slight or intense, or whether it's short-lived or lasts for years, the following ideas can help you temper your feelings for your own peace of mind as well as your child's benefit.

• **Accept that some separation anxiety is healthy.** Don't try to eliminate all your feelings of separation anxiety. These emotions exist for very good reasons. First, they will guide you as you make choices about when and how to leave your child. They will help you decide if you are choosing the right caregiver and the right setting. They can also keep you close to your child so that you will know if something is wrong or troubling him.

The pain you feel when you are apart is an integral element of the intense love you carry in your heart for your child. It is a defining part of your relationship that makes it rise head and shoulders above all other relationships that your child will have in his life. I have learned that teenagers who have parents with this kind of deep, fervent love stay closer to the family over time, and they come through the typical challenges of the teen years much easier. So don't wish away all your heartfelt tenderness—it is an important part of being a loving parent.

Professional-Speak

"Your anguish at being away from your child will convey itself, but it is part of your caring. Recognizing these feelings will bring the two of you closer."

—T. Berry Brazelton, M.D., author of *Touchpoints: Birth to Three*

- **Acknowledge that some separation is a good thing for your child.** It's likely that a part of your anxiety is based on the feeling that you can take care of your child better than anyone else can. And you know what? That's probably true! However, even if other caregivers don't do things exactly as you do, it's more than likely that your child will adapt and accept these differences. Furthermore, your child's world will be filled with people other than you, and it's a wonderful growing experience for him to learn that *different* does not mean *bad*. Actually, it will be much easier for him to learn this now than when he gets older, so bask in the opportunity for his sake.

- **Get busy!** As much as you may miss your child when you are apart, this is a great opportunity to do things that are more easily accomplished without a child attached to your hip. So don't let the hours pass by nonchalantly, and don't spend them absorbed in worry or guilt. Make use of the time in a healthy and productive way. Go for a jog, take a bike ride, go out to lunch, clean your closet, get a manicure, or go shopping. Create a schedule of what you'll do while

Alyssa, twenty-two months old, and Mikaela, three years old

your child is gone, so you don't find yourself undecided and lacking the motivation to *do* something.

If your child will be gone for large amounts of time on a regular basis, such as after a divorce, plan to use those times in a fruitful way. Join a health club, take a class, join a mother's club, start music lessons, learn to paint, write a book, or start a hobby. Create a to-do list or a wish-to-do list, and keep it posted in a visible place. When you find yourself wandering aimlessly through the house, pick something from your list and get busy!

• **Rely on friendships.** You may have had more time for your friends before children entered your life; it's common that adult friendships lose out when young children arrive on the scene. This is an important time for you to rekindle and nurture those relationships that may have fallen by the wayside. Friends who also have young children can be helpful as they likely have feelings similar to yours. Friends with older children are like gold because they likely have lived through this phase and have the wisdom of experience. Friends without children have important value because they can pull you out of your child-centered existence for a short time and draw you into activities and conversation that don't revolve around parenting topics.

• **Curb your nervousness around your child.** Children are remarkably perceptive. If you are anxious and worried about your separation from your child, then she may create worries based on your modeling. Avoid repeated declarations of love. Don't make passionate promises of a rapid return. Instead, do your best to be cheerful and relaxed at times of separation. Save your worried face, if you still have one, until the door between you closes.

• **Plan something for the two of you to look forward to.** Set up an activity or even a chunk of casual playtime for when you and your child are reunited. When you set up something specific, you'll enjoy thinking about the pleasure you'll share at that time. Having a specific purpose in mind lets you anticipate a precise end to the separation and frees you up to do other things until the prearranged event.

Sometimes when parents are away from their children, they feel a tug of guilt that when they were together, they didn't take advantage of the time. They were busy tending to other things and not really spending as much time as they should have engaged with their child. (That's called life.) However, when you plan an activity to make the most of your time together, you will find that you can relax more and even enjoy your time apart. This idea can also help your child weather the separation, as she too will have special time with you to look forward to.

7

Extreme Emotions: Separation Anxiety Disorder

Separation anxiety can be very challenging for families. There's no doubt it's a difficult situation when your child cries, clings, and has tantrums as you attempt to peel him off your leg. A tearful good-bye at the door or a sorrowful face at the window can pull at any parent's heartstrings. However, with information, tips, and solutions, most parents and children can work through this inevitable rite of passage. Separation anxiety is a normal stage for most children, and this book contains many suggestions for helping to nudge your child through the process of managing and overcoming this stage.

While typical separation anxiety can have some intense moments, there are children who cross the line from normal anxiety to an actual medical problem referred to as *separation anxiety disorder (SAD)*, which has more extreme and longer-lasting effects. This disorder requires a

Professional-Speak

"Anxiety is a vaguely defined and commonly used word that also has a strict scientific meaning. In mental health research the word *anxiety* describes the thoughts, feelings, and behaviors that occur when a person has the perception of serious danger in situations where other people do not perceive danger. Anxiety means worrying that something really, really bad might happen at any minute."

—Elizabeth DuPont Spencer, M.S.W., Robert L. DuPont, M.D., and Caroline M. DuPont, M.D., authors of
The Anxiety Cure for Kids: A Guide for Parents

professional's diagnosis and guidance to help your child overcome his anxiety.

Separation Anxiety Disorder

Children with SAD may be resistant to the ideas presented in this book. You may try for months and find little or no relief for your child's suffering. Children with normal separation anxiety may have some similar behaviors as those with the more extreme disorder, but their behavior will improve over a period of a month or two when you follow a No-Cry plan. Anytime you are concerned about your child, of course, you should follow your instincts and talk to a professional. The following checklists can help you determine if your child needs expert intervention on this issue and can also serve as tools to share with your health care professional as you take steps toward resolving your child's separation anxiety problems.

Children who exhibit the following common signs of SAD may benefit from a more structured plan, plus counseling that is organized by a professional:

- Tremendous fear of being alone
- Panic and distress that occurs when a parent leaves the room or the house
- Crying upon separation that continues off and on until a parent's return
- Need for constant physical contact with a parent, such as clinging, holding, and shadowing
- Clinginess that prevents normal play and socializing with other children
- Persistent worry about getting lost and separated from a parent
- Excessive worry about a parent dying or becoming sick or hurt
- Unwarranted complaints of physical symptoms, such as stomachaches or headaches
- Worries and stresses about separation even before it happens
- Refusal to sleep alone after being able to sleep by himself in the past
- Frequent nightmares about separation situations or danger

- New anxiety that develops after a life event and doesn't dissipate, such as after a hospital stay, the death of a loved one or pet, or a move to a new home
- Persistent, intense reluctance or refusal to attend daycare or school, or frequent excuses to stay home due to fear of separation from the home or parent
- Refusal to play at other children's homes or attend field trips, parties, or other events (in a child over six or seven years old)
- Symptoms that persist or worsen in severity even after trying various ideas and solutions presented in this book for a month or more
- A parent with current anxiety disorders or who suffered from separation anxiety disorder as a child

Key Point

Almost all children have some normal separation anxiety between the ages of six months and six years. Separation anxiety disorder affects approximately 4–6 percent of children between the ages of six and eleven years, and about 1–2 percent of teenagers; it is found in boys and girls equally. SAD very rarely persists into adulthood, and the rate of full recovery is very high.

How Separation Anxiety Disorder Is Treated

There are a number of ways to treat SAD. The right method is different for each child and family situation. Here are some of the techniques commonly used to treat separation anxiety disorder:

- **Play therapy.** A trained professional uses toys, puppets, games, or art to help a child express her feelings and learn new ways of handling her fears.
- **Family therapy.** The parents and therapist form a team and create a plan to work with the child.

Kayleigh, eighteen months old

- **Cognitive behavioral therapy.** This method is used for older children and involves one-on-one sessions with a counselor. Through a series of sessions, the child learns how to control anxious thoughts and behaviors and learns to use coping skills.
- **Alternative therapies.** There are a variety of options for families who lean toward alternative health care options. Anxiety disorders can be treated with acupuncture, meditation, massage therapy, and biofeedback.

Where to Get More Help

If you suspect that your child may have SAD, it's wise to call a professional who specializes in working with children. This person can help you determine if your child would benefit from a treatment plan. Your first call can be to your pediatrician or regular health care provider for a discussion and description of symptoms. Your doctor can rule out any physical health problems as the source of anxiety and provide a recommendation to a mental health professional. Be sure to consider all of the options open to your child. The following organizations can also provide you with information and guidance:

American Academy of Child and Adolescent Psychiatry
www.aacap.org

American Academy of Pediatrics
www.aap.org

Anxiety Disorders Association of America (ADAA)
www.adaa.org

Your child's pediatrician, daycare, church, school, or school district may also have recommendations.

Books for Parents

A number of books have been written for parents about SAD. These are good references if you are unsure whether your child needs further help or if you wish to be better informed during the process of working with a professional.

Chansky, Tamar E. *Freeing Your Child from Anxiety: Powerful, Practical Solutions to Overcome Your Child's Fears, Worries, and Phobias.* New York: Broadway Books, 2004.

Eisen, Andrew R., Linda B. Engler, and Joshua Sparrow. *Helping Your Child Overcome Separation Anxiety or School Refusal: A Step-by-Step Guide for Parents.* Oakland, CA: New Harbinger Publications, 2006.

Spencer, Elizabeth DuPont, Robert L. DuPont, and Caroline M. DuPont. *The Anxiety Cure for Kids: A Guide for Parents.* Hoboken, NJ: J. Wiley, 2003.

Index

Adult separation anxiety
 questionnaire, 136
Adults-only vacations, planning,
 117–20
Advance visits, separations and, 57
"Alone time," permitting, for babies
 and toddlers, 27
Annoyance, avoiding showing, 70–71
Anxiety, things that increase overall,
 76. *See also* Separation anxiety;
 Stranger anxiety
Attachment, 6
Attitudes, leaving child and, 29
Autonomy, creating baby steps for, 56

Babies, no-cry solutions for, 21. *See also*
 New babies
 allowing separations that the child
  initiates, 32–33
 avoiding excess separation, 38–39
 avoiding in-arms transfers, 24–25
 avoiding prolonged partings, 28
 avoiding rushed partings, 28
 avoiding sneaking away, 28
 babying, 25
 creating baby steps of autonomy,
  55–56
 cueing caregiver's response, 31
 encouraging relationships with
  transitional objects, 33–34
 expressing cheerful, positive attitude
  when leaving, 29
 having child well rested and well
  fed, 37–38
 having dress rehearsals, 55–56
 having practice sessions, 30–31
 introducing new people, 35–37
 introducing people gently, 34–35
 inviting distractions, 31–32
 minimizing separations, 26–27
 monitoring responses of parents, 39
 permitting "alone time," 27
 playing bye-bye game, 23
 playing peek-a-boo with objects, 22
 playing peek-a-boo with people, 23

practicing separations, 24
 telling babies what to expect, 27–28
Babysitters
 preparing house for, 76
 tips for when child resists, 87–92
Bedside pets, 109
Bedtime separation anxiety, 63
 tips for, 105–12
Bedwetting, managing, and sleepovers,
 116
Blankets, encouraging relationships
 with security, 33–34
Bond, Felicia, 67
Bonding, 6
Books about similar situations, reading,
 59
Bracelets. *See* Magic Bracelets
Brazelton, T. Berry, 100
Bubble blowing, 74–75
Business travel, tips for handling,
 126–27
Bye-bye games, playing, 1

Call-home plans, 117
Children's books about similar
 situations, 59, 81–83
Chill times, providing, 63
Clinging, setting limits on, 77
Coping techniques. *See* Relaxation and
 coping techniques
Crawford, Mark, 54

Dacey, John S., 61, 65
Daddy/Mommy box, 12
Diaries, helping children keep, 123
Distractions, inviting, when leaving,
 31–32
Divorces, tips for handling, 123–26
Door game, 83
Dress rehearsals, for separations, 55–56
DuPont, Caroline M., 141
DuPont, Robert L., 141

Eating schedules, maintaining, 61–62
Eisen, Andrew R., 4, 74, 107, 115

Embarrassment, separation anxiety and, 16
Emotionally safe children, keeping, 13–14
Engler, Linda B., 115
Escolar, Maria Luisa, 33
Experience, lack of, separation anxiety and, 15

Fay, Jim, 108
Fear, separation anxiety and, 15–16
Fight-or-flight reaction, 2–3
Fiore, Lisa B., 61, 65
First grade, tips for sending child to, 100–103
Forehand, Rex, 124
Frustrations, avoiding showing, 70–71

Games
    playing bye-bye, 1
    playing door, 83
    playing peek-a-boo with objects, 22
    playing peek-a-boo with people, 23
    playing separation, 52
    playing What-If, 66–67
Good-byes, morning, 96–100

Hobey, Paige, 93
Homeostatic sleep pressure, 62
Honesty, separation anxiety and, 79

"If You Give" books, 67
In-arms transfers, avoiding, 24–25, 89
Independent play, encouraging, 75

Kindergarten, tips for sending child to, 100–103
Kissing Hand, The (Penn), 99

Leach, Penelope, 26
Lifestyle changes, separation anxiety and, 15
Long, Nicholas, 124
Love, separation anxiety and, 1
Loveys, encouraging relationships with, 33–34, 109
Lucky charms, giving, 56

Magic Bracelet, 41–43, 124
    finding bracelet to use as, 43–44
    introducing child to, 45–46
    magic words for, 47–48
    put-away routine for, 48–49

sending child to kindergarten or first grade and, 102–3
    tips for, 46–47
    using, 47, 49
    weaning child from, 49–50
Meal times, maintaining schedules for, 61–62
Military duty, tips for handling, 120–23
Morning good-byes, 96–100
Morning routines, establishing, 2

New babies, tips for handling arrival of, and siblings, 103–5. *See also* Babies
New people, 71
    introducing babies and toddlers to, 35–37
    introducing preschool and school-age children to, 54
No-cry process, for peaceful problem solving, 19–20
No-cry solutions
    for babies and toddlers, 21
        allowing separations that the child initiates, 32–33
        avoiding excess separation, 38–39
        avoiding in-arms transfers, 24–25
        avoiding prolonged partings, 28
        avoiding rushed partings, 28
        avoiding sneaking away, 28
        babying, 25
        creating baby steps of autonomy, 55–56
        cueing caregiver's response, 31
        encouraging relationships with transitional objects, 33–34
        express cheerful, positive attitude when leaving, 29
        having child well-rested and well-fed, 37–38
        having dress rehearsals, 55–56
        having practice sessions, 30–31
        introducing new people, 35–37
        introducing people gently, 34–35

inviting distractions, 31–32
minimizing separations,
26–27
monitoring responses of
parents, 39
permitting "alone time," 27
playing bye-bye game, 23
playing peek-a-boo with
objects, 22
playing peek-a-boo with
people, 23
practicing separations, 24
telling babies and toddlers
what to expect, 27–28
for preschool and school-age
children, 51
acknowledging child's
feelings, 59–61
allowing child to bring
along something, 70
allowing child to leave
you, 70
allowing warm-up periods,
54
arranging playdates with
friends, 64
avoiding planting worry
seeds, 58
avoiding showing
annoyance, frustration,
or worry, 70–71
creating baby steps of
autonomy, 55–56
downplaying one's return,
77
encouraging independent
play, 75
encouraging positive
thoughts, 64–66
giving calming trinkets, 56
giving choices, 68
giving photos of parents, 59
giving promises to return,
53
having relaxed morning
routines, 64
having reunion routines, 58
having specific parting
routines, 57–58
informing child what to
expect, 52–53
introducing new people
gradually, 54

maintaining child's sleep
and eating schedules,
61–62
playing separation games, 52
playing What-If game,
66–67
providing chill times, 63
reading children's books
about similar situations,
59
recognizing it's not a now-
or-never choice, 69
relaxation and coping
techniques, 73–75
sending funny faces, 59
talking to teachers or
caregivers, 70
telling stories that teach, 55
using prayer to help child
cope, 68–69
visiting in advance, 57
watching out for red flags,
78–79
Now-or-never choices, avoiding, 69
Numeroff, Laura Joffe, 67

Packer, Leslie E., 77
Paper Hug, A (Skolomoski), 123
Parenting, being observant and
flexible, 79
Parents
monitoring responses of, 1
personal separation anxiety stories
of, 131–35
tips for, who can't leave rooms,
82–86
tips for, who feel separation anxiety,
137–41
Parties
attending, children and, 112–14
tips for attending, 114–17
Partings. *See also* Separations
avoiding prolonged, 28
avoiding rushed, 28
playmate, 128–29
Peek-a-boo games
with objects, 22
with people, 23
Penn, Audrey, 99
Pets, bedside, 109
Playdates, attending, children and,
112–14
Playmate partings, 128–29

Positive thoughts, encouraging, 64–66
Prayer, for helping children cope,
  68–69
Preschool children, no-cry solutions
  for, 51
  acknowledging child's feelings,
    59–61
  allowing child to bring along
    something, 70
  allowing child to leave you, 70
  allowing warm-up periods, 54
  arranging playdates with friends, 64
  avoiding planting worry seeds, 58
  avoiding showing annoyance,
    frustration, or worry, 70–71
  creating baby steps of autonomy,
    55–56
  downplaying one's return, 77
  encouraging independent play, 75
  encouraging positive thoughts,
    64–66
  giving calming trinket to, 56
  giving choices, 68
  giving photos of parents, 59
  giving promises to return, 53
  having dress rehearsals, 55–56
  having relaxed morning routines,
    64
  having reunion routines, 58
  having specific parting routines,
    57–58
  informing child what to expect,
    52–53
  introducing new people gradually,
    54
  maintaining child's sleep and eating
    schedules, 61–62
  playing separation games, 52
  playing What-If game, 66–67
  providing chill times, 63
  reading children's books about
    similar situations, 59
  recognizing it's not a now-or-never
    choice, 69
  relaxation and coping techniques,
    73–75
  sending funny faces, 59
  talking to teachers or caregivers, 70
  telling stories that teach, 55
  using prayer to help child cope,
    68–69
  visiting in advance, 57
  watching out for red flags, 78–79

Problem solving, no-cry process for, 19
Put-away routine, for Magic Bracelet,
  48–49

Quiet Bunny, 73–74

Red flags, watching out for, 78–79
Relaxation and coping techniques,
  73–75
Remarrying, tips for handling, 123–26
Return/reunion routines, establishing,
  57–58
Room, tips for when parent can't leave,
  82–86
Routines, having specific, 94–95

SAD. *See* Separation anxiety disorder
  (SAD)
Schaefer, Charles E., 107
School-age children, no-cry solutions
  for, 51
  acknowledging child's feelings,
    59–61
  allowing child to bring along
    something, 70
  allowing child to leave you, 70
  allowing warm-up periods, 54
  arranging playdates with friends, 64
  avoiding planting worry seeds, 58
  avoiding showing annoyance,
    frustration, or worry, 70–71
  creating baby steps of autonomy,
    55–56
  downplaying one's return, 77
  encouraging independent play, 75
  encouraging positive thoughts,
    64–66
  giving calming trinket to, 56
  giving choices, 68
  giving photos of parents, 59
  giving promises to return, 53
  having dress rehearsals, 55–56
  having relaxed morning routines, 64
  having reunion routines, 58
  having specific parting routines,
    57–58
  informing child what to expect,
    52–53
  introducing new people gradually,
    54
  maintaining child's sleep and eating
    schedules, 61–62
  playing separation games, 52

playing What-If game, 66–67
providing chill times, 63
reading children's books about
    similar situations, 59
recognizing it's not a now-or-never
    choice, 69
relaxation and coping techniques,
    73–75
sending funny faces, 59
talking to teachers or caregivers, 70
telling stories that teach, 55
using prayer to help child cope,
    68–69
visiting in advance, 57
watching out for red flags, 78–79
Security blankets, encouraging
    relationships with, 33–34
Separation anxiety
    bedtime, 63, 105–12
    causes of, 3–5
    chart, signs and symptoms, 9–10
    children in early years and, 2, 4
    children who don't have, 12–13
    defined, 1
    determining child's level of, 5
    determining if it's a problem, 16–19
    embarrassment and, 16
    emotions and, 15–16
    factors determining child's level of, 5
    fear and, 15–16
    honesty and, 79
    lifestyle changes and, 15
    love and, 1
    origin of, 1
    parents' emotions, 11
    parents' personal stories of, 131–35
    reasons for, 2–3
    shyness and, 15
    signs and symptoms, 9–10
    situations that masquerade as,
        15–16
    slow adaptation and, 15
    symptoms of, 8–11
    tips for parents who feel, 137–41
    understanding age-appropriateness
        of, 53–54
    unpredictability of, 11
    worry and, 16
Separation anxiety disorder (SAD)
    children with, 141–43
    information and guidance resources
        for, 144–45
    treating, 143–44

Separations. *See also* Partings
    avoiding excess, 38–39
    determining timing for, 14
    dress rehearsals for, 55–56
    lack of experience and, 15
    Magic Bracelet for, 41–50
    minimizing, 26–27
    practice sessions for, 30–31
    practicing, for babies and toddlers,
        24
    reflecting on previous successful, 72
Shyness, separation anxiety and, 15
Siblings
    difficulty handling arrival of a new
        baby, 103–5
    when older siblings go off to school,
        128–29
Sick days, children and, 103
Sitters. *See* Babysitters
Skolomoski, Stephanie, 123
Sleep schedules, maintaining, 61–62
Sleepovers, attending, 114–17
Sneaking away, avoiding, 28
Solo play, 33
Spencer, Elizabeth DuPont, 141
Stories that teach, telling, 55
Stranger anxiety, 5–6
    age for appearance of, 6
    duration of, 6–7
    helping child overcome, 7
Strangers. *See* New people

Tammeus, William D., 3
Test parent survey, 135–37
Tips
    for attending parties, 114–17
    for attending sleepovers, 114–17
    for bedtime separation anxiety,
        105–12
    for handling arrival of new baby and
        siblings, 103–5
    for handling business travel,
        126–27
    for handling divorces, 123–26
    for handling military duty, 120–23
    for introducing Magic Bracelet,
        46–47
    for parents, who feel separation
        anxiety, 137–41
    for planning adults-only vacations,
        117–20
    for sending child to kindergarten or
        first grade, 100–103

for when child resists babysitter,
87–92
for when mom or dad goes to work,
92–96
for when parent can't leave room,
82–86
Toddlers, no-cry solutions for, 21
allowing separations that the child
initiates, 32–33
avoiding excess separation, 38–39
avoiding in-arms transfers, 24–25
avoiding prolonged partings, 28
avoiding rushed partings, 28
avoiding sneaking away, 28
babying, 25
creating baby steps of autonomy,
55–56
cueing caregiver's response, 31
encouraging relationships with
transitional objects, 33–34
expressing cheerful, positive attitude
when leaving, 29
having child well rested and well
fed, 37–38
having dress rehearsals, 55–56
having practice sessions, 30–31
introducing new people, 35–37

introducing people gently, 34–35
inviting distractions, 31–32
minimizing separations, 26–27
monitoring responses of parents,
39
permitting "alone time," 27
playing bye-bye game, 23
playing peek-a-boo with objects, 22
playing peek-a-boo with people, 23
practicing separations, 24
telling toddlers what to expect,
27–28
Touchpoints (Brazelton), 100
Transitional objects, encouraging
relationships with, 33–34. *See also*
Magic Bracelet

Vacations, planning adults-only,
117–20

What-If game, 66–67
Work, tips for when mom or dad goes
to, 92–96
Worries
avoiding showing, 70–71
separation anxiety and, 16
Worry seeds, avoiding planting, 58

About the Author

Parenting educator Elizabeth Pantley is president of Better Beginnings, Inc., a family resource and education company. She frequently speaks to parents at schools, hospitals, and parent groups around the world. Her presentations are received with enthusiasm and praised as realistic, warm, and helpful.

She is a regular radio-show guest, and she is frequently quoted as a parenting expert in newspapers and magazines such as *Parents*, *Parenting*, *Woman's Day*, *Mother & Baby*, *Today's Parent*, and *Good Housekeeping* and on hundreds of parent-directed websites. She publishes a newsletter, *Parent Tips*, which is distributed in schools, doctor's offices, and parent programs everywhere.

Elizabeth is the author of these popular parenting books, available in twenty-four languages:

The No-Cry Sleep Solution
The No-Cry Sleep Solution for Toddlers and Preschoolers
The No-Cry Potty Training Solution
The No-Cry Nap Solution
The No-Cry Discipline Solution
Gentle Baby Care
Hidden Messages
Perfect Parenting
Kid Cooperation

She was also a contributing author, with Dr. William and Martha Sears, to *The Successful Child*.

Elizabeth and her husband, Robert, live in Washington State, along with their four children—Angela, Vanessa, David, and Coleton—and Grama (Elizabeth's mother). Elizabeth is an involved participant in her children's school and sports activities and has served in positions as varied as softball coach and school PTA president.

For more information, excerpts, parenting articles, and contests, visit the author's website at www.nocrysolution.com.

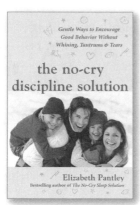